The Englishman
of the Peseta

THE ENGLISHMAN OF THE PESETA

THE LIFE AND TIMES OF
GEORGE LANGWORTHY

Mike Shapton

The Englishman of the Peseta
Mike Shapton

Published by Aspect Design, 2020

Designed, printed and bound by Aspect Design
89 Newtown Road, Malvern, Worcs. WR14 1PD
United Kingdom
Tel: 01684 561567
E-mail: allan@aspect-design.net
Website: www.aspect-design.net

A copy of this book has been deposited
with the British Library Board

ISBN 978-1-912078-78-3

For Gill, Laura, Rachel and Naomi,
with my love always.

CONTENTS

Illustrations. ix

Note on Footnotes. xiii

Acknowledgements xv

Introduction 1

Chapter One   A Village in Mourning. 5

Chapter Two   Cottonopolis 9

Chapter Three   Uppingham and Manliness. 20

Chapter Four   Horses, Hounds and Fusiliers. 34

Chapter Five   A Family Scandal. 44

Chapter Six   India 60

Chapter Seven   England and Marriage 81

Chapter Eight   South Africa. 89

Chapter Nine   Málaga and Santa Clara 107

Chapter Ten   El Inglés de la Peseta 136

Chapter Eleven   War and a Kind of Peace 165

Chapter Twelve   George's Legacy 182

Chapter Thirteen   Travellers, Settlers, Artists and Tourists 186

Appendix I   Mercedes Beautell, Memories from Her Youth . . . 199

Appendix II   Extracts from 'El Indolente' by Luis Cernuda . . . 207

Appendix III   Extract from the *Pall Mall Gazette*, 1887. 217

Appendix IV   Extract from the *Black Horse Gazette*, 1910 221

General Bibliography. 229

ILLUSTRATIONS

Memorial plaque in Torremolinos. 2

The entrance to the English Cemetery in Málaga. 6

The inscription on the sepulchre of Consul William Mark. 7

A view of the graves of George and Annie 8

Drawing of Greengate Mills 11

Ernest Rutherford with Hans Geiger. 17

Sketch of Uppingham 20

Edward Thring mid 1860s. 21

Uppingham's old school house. 24

Cambrian Hotel yard and school room 26

Old Constables, 1862. 28

A game of fives 29

The original fives court at Eton College. 30

Uppingham School 'Dateline' by J. Rudman 32

The Headmistresses' Conference, 11 June 1887 33

A typical court scene c.1900. 54

'How to Help Mrs Langworthy', *Pall Mall Gazette*, 11 May 1887. 55

'Advertisements & Notices', *Pall Mall Gazette*, 26 May 1887. 57

Sketch 7th Dragoon Guards entering the Suez Canal in 1882. 62

Members of the regiment on horse in front of Sphinx, 1882 62

Bungalow Umballa. Courtesy of the British Library. 65

Cantonment Umballa. Courtesy of the British Library. 67

Map of part of India showing principal towns and railways 68

Camp at Aligarh 69

Annie with her older sister, Frances, in India. 72

A young Annie 72

Charles and Elizabeth Roe with family and friends 73

Racecourse at Secunderabad 75

Officers of the 7th Dragoon at Aligarh camp, 1891. 77

The 7th Dragoons on parade at Aligarh 78
George the swordsman. 80
A studio portrait of Annie 81
7th Dragoons regimental dress uniform, 1837 and 1897 82
George's yacht Sayonara, 1895 83
Regimental staghounds, 1896. 83
Officers on Salisbury Plain, 1897 84
Park Lodge 85
Knightsbridge Barracks, Hyde Park side 85
Annie in her wedding dress 86
Holy Trinity, Knightsbridge 88
Certificate of marriage. 88
Horses being embarked at Southampton 91
George 'captain for the day'. 91
SS Armenian leaving Southampton 8 February 1900. 92
Entraining horses 92
Private Best 94
Captain G. Langworthy leading 'B' Squadron across Parys Drift 95
From a sketch made at the time of the Battle of Diamond Hill. 97
George relaxing 98
George's dog Toby tangles with a monkey 98
Map of significant places in George's experience in S. Africa 100
Officers of 'O' battery and 7th Dragoons. 101
George at Harrismith 103
A Blockhouse. 104
Málaga port. 107
The Roe family home in Lahore. 116
George at the Villa in Málaga 116
Santa Clara from La Carihuela beach. 118
Main house under reconstruction 120
The completed house. 120
George's boat. 122
Planting in front of the main house. 122
George poses with a hunting party. 122
Planting in front of the main house. 122
Developed land around cuartel 122

Staff ready the dogs for an expedition 123

Waiting to shoot. 124

A picnic in woods 124

Annie, George and a friend with some of their dogs. 125

Annie and her sister on a donkey ride 125

Receiving guests at Santa Clara 126

Annie and George, possibly with relatives 126

A motor car in difficulty 127

The Star, on the left, and the De Dion-Bouton. 127

A send-off from the village children. 127

Enjoying tea on the verandah. 129

Enjoying tea on the verandah. 129

A shady corner with friend and dogs 130

The tennis court. 130

Annie 131

Annie in mantilla. 131

Inscription on Annie's grave. 132

George in his First World War major's uniform 133

Image of George's silver badge award. 134

A view of Santa Clara from the sea. 135

Eddy's statement from a text owned by George 137

An example of a Tratamiento. 140

George moved to a simple room. 141

The dedication to George. 141

A silver peseta.. 142

A relaxed George 144

George with his sister Ida, her husband and child 145

The entrance to the hotel 147

The Beautells and friends. 150

Pedlar and donkey at the entrance 151

Path up to the entrance 151

A bedroom in the hotel 152

The most seaward of the miradores 152

The hotel veranda 152

A sitting room in the hotel. 152

Santa Clara from the air 153

Diving off the headland. 153

Swimming off the headland. 153

The *Graf Zeppelin* over Santa Clara, 1931 154

A group of Oxford students wait for the bus to Algeciras 154

Santa Clara from the sea 154

Aerial photo of the hotel and grounds 155

Sketch of Santa Clara as a hotel. 155

Promotional leaflet 156

Salvador Dalí and Gala 158

A couple enjoy the solitude of a mirador 160

A studio portrait of Denise Robins c.1960 .161

Karey Lierneux at Santa Clara 1932 161

Views of La Carihuela beach 163

Young supporters of the government mobilise in 1936. 168

Damage in Málaga at the start of the war 169

British citizens await embarkation 25 July 1936. 170

Map of Andalucía in August 1936. 172

Sir Peter Chalmers-Mitchell. 174

Villa Santa Lucía, Málaga 174

Málaga after the entrance of troops February 1937 176

The Spanish, British and US flags fly above Santa Clara. 179

George Langworthy, his last studio portrait. 180

Maria Campoy with her husband Manuel and children 182

Dedication to Margaret Beautell 184

Mercedes in 1930 199

Luis Cernuda with Lorca and Aleixandre 207

The 20-hp Star, built in Wolverhampton 222

Note on Footnotes

Although one important function of the footnotes is to give credit to the main written sources of my information, I am not intending full academic-style referencing as the book is not written in that manner. The bibliography contains sufficient detail for readers who are interested in further reading to locate most of the material. The Internet yielded a host of information from census returns to the location of obscure documents which would have been difficult to discover, never mind access without spending a lot more time and money. I have not referenced most of these sites.

ACKNOWLEDGEMENTS

My search for the story of George led me first to Remi Fernández Campoy. Although Remi never knew George personally, she continues to celebrate his memory and provided me with invaluable information and privileged access to her collection of photographs inherited from her family and from George. I would like to thank, too, the descendants of Margaret Beautell, especially Carlos Beautell González who supplied photographs, and Gabriela Martinez-Arroyo Beautell who gave me permission to reproduce her mother's reminiscences of George and Santa Clara. Thanks to Major Graeme Green and his staff at the York Army Museum, the regimental museum of The Royal Dragoon Guards and The Yorkshire Regiment, who gave me ready access to the museum archive and supplied photographs both from the regimental gazette and a personal album of a contemporary of George's in the regiment. I am grateful to Jerry Rudman, archivist at Uppingham School, again for supplying photos and access to a history of the school, but also for a guided tour of parts of the school which would have been familiar to George.

Thanks also to Penrose Scott, secretary to the estate of Denise Robins for supplying the photograph of the Denise.

Several other institutions and individuals have offered me information and guidance. Of these I would like to mention: Dr Gareth Stockey, associate professor, University of Nottingham;

Professor Simon Gunn, University of Leicester; Belinda Day, Senior Curator, Collections Development and Review at the National Army Museum; and Revd Peter Kettle, Assistant Priest, Holy Trinity, Prince Consort Road, Knightsbridge, London.

I would like to thank friends who have supported me in different ways, starting with my wife Gill who agreed with me on that day in 2010 that it would be interesting to research George . . . and has enjoyed the research in York, Torremolinos and Málaga. Thank you, especially, Gill, for creating the maps. Chris Ford painstakingly enhanced the photos from Remi, and Jeanette Leyland helped with the typing. Dave Wiltshire supported me in early communications and on my first trip to Torremolinos (his Spanish is better than mine). Vicki Lloyd and Mark Doel read drafts and offered invaluable advice and Mark designed the family tree.

Of course, I take responsibility for all errors and omissions. I have endeavoured to acknowledge the sources of all photographs and seek permission for their use.

It is a cruel irony that the people of Torremolinos with whom George shared his wealth could look across a narrow stretch of sea to Africa. That had been the home of the slaves who worked the cotton plantations of the USA. In due course their produce was turned into goods by the workers who lived in the squalor of Salford. Those goods lay the foundation of the Langworthy wealth, some of which came so close to the shores of Africa.

INTRODUCTION

Why would a man brought up in the prosperous comfort of a nineteenth-century Manchester cotton-manufacturing and merchant family spend his final days, by his own choice, almost penniless, amongst the fishing folk of the Spanish Mediterranean coast? This is the question I asked myself as I began to look into the life of George Langworthy.

Quite by chance I had read an article in an English language newspaper on the Costa del Sol in 2010. The headline read:

THE GENEROUS EXPAT BRIT WHO CHANGED THE FACE OF TORREMOLINOS.

The subtitle read:

The grandfather of Costa del Sol tourism, George Langworthy, died penniless and heartbroken – but much adored.

I was surprised that I had never heard of him. This book represents my search for this 'generous expat' and is my attempt to answer the question I pose above. It is the the story of 'don Jorge' as he was known to the locals in Torremolinos or, as he may have preferred you to call him, Major George Langworthy of the 7th, (Princess Royals) Dragoon Guards. If you were in the city of

Memorial plaque in Torremolinos.
Copyright © Mike Shapton

Salford you might find yourself in a district called Langworthy, centred on Langworthy Road and Langworthy Park. You might even get on or off a metro tram at the stop called Langworthy. These and other commemorations of the Langworthy name do not, however, celebrate the subject of this book even though they are linked to it.

To find lasting tributes to George Langworthy, and they are less conspicuous, you need to fly almost 1,200 miles south to Málaga and make your way just a few kilometres west to Torremolinos, a journey numerous Mancunians have made. Behind the headland which divides the two main beaches of El Bajondillo and La Carihuela you will find Calle del Castillo del Inglés (Street of the Englishman's Castle). Underneath one street plaque you will find another which says (in translation) 'In memory of George Langworthy, adopted favourite son of Torremolinos'. The street will lead you to the modern apartment building known as 'Castillo Santa Clara'. In the gardens you can find memorial plaques to George, in his military uniform, and his wife Annie.

Now that I know so much more about him I would question whether he died as heartbroken as the newspaper article suggested. As you will read, his time with his wife in Spain was sadly limited, but for another thirty years he would enjoy the delights of his adopted Mediterranean home marred only by his return to England in the First World War and the tragedy of the Spanish Civil War twenty years later. I have no doubt that the loss of his wife will have been an enormous sadness at the time, but through it he seems to have found an inner peace which is central to how loved and respected he came to be by the local people.

In 2014, two authors from Málaga published two books, one a work of fiction, *El Hotel del Inglés*, based around the 'life' of the hotel into which George's home was converted and a briefer book containing information gleaned by them from local sources on the Costa del Sol about the life of George and his wife. The knowledge it offered about his life prior to arriving in Spain was limited and I resolved to learn more.

George and Annie had no children and the rest of the Manchester family from which he came produced no sons bearing the name Langworthy, to the best of my knowledge. One of the challenges of researching and writing this book is that George and Annie left nothing in writing apart from an account of a motoring trip that George wrote for his regimental gazette. Another difficulty was that the records of most British army officers serving before the First World War were lost in a fire in the Second World War. Fortunately the couple did leave a small archive of photographs, some of which I have had the privilege to view, copy and include in this book with the current owner's permission. Other photographs help fill in the story, from sources as diverse as his regiment's museum to the descendants of the people who first successfully ran the hotel. Another piece of good luck is that Langworthy is an uncommon name, so it has been comparatively easy to locate documentary information gleaned from the Internet (census returns etc.). To give a wider context to his life I have drawn on a number of sources as diverse as regimental publications and a romantic novel. Most of the material is from writers in English, some of them contemporary to George, and I hope the direct quotations from them help capture the flavour of the time when George lived. Advice from current academics and writers with interests relevant to the locations where George spent parts of his life has helped me understand context where this has been helpful.

Unlike future generations of Mancunians, George never flew from Manchester to Málaga. His intervening military journey took him via India, Egypt and South Africa. His temporal journey took him from the heyday of Victorian Manchester to the first shoots of the mass tourism of the Spanish 'costas' which helped revitalise the crippled Spanish economy after the devastating Civil War of 1936–9.

I hope you will enjoy accompanying me in the process of discovery. I am not a professional historian, nor do I have a military background, so I may explain things that the reader already understands. I have however had a great interest in Spain since starting to learn the language over fifty years ago and subsequently studying the literature and history of the country and living in Andalucía for most of a year shortly thereafter.

Researching George's life has felt like armchair detective work, hugely enjoyable. It is often recognised that history comes to life when it is possible to personalise it and George's presence in Britain and parts of its Empire and in Spain before it became a mass tourist destination has brought those areas to life for me.

                                                        Mike Shapton, 2020

CHAPTER ONE
A Village in Mourning

If you happen to be in Málaga and find yourself in need of a peaceful oasis away from the bustle of the city centre you could do worse than take a stroll along the Paseo Reding, until you find yourself at a gateway on which is written 'St George's Anglican Church'. You are walking parallel to the Mediterranean which you might glimpse between buildings as you walk. It can be a cooling walk even on a hot day as the trees on the Paseo give so much shade. On the way you are likely to have passed the flamboyant neo-baroque extravagance of the Ayuntamiento (town hall) on Paseo del Parque. As you enter Paseo Reding the Plaza de Toros (bullring) is on your right. The buildings of the Paseo give a fine impression of Málaga's nineteenth-century wealth, while above them tower the walls of the eleventh-century Moorish Alcazaba. Just as you reach the entrance to St George's your eye might be distracted by the magnificence of the Gran Hotel Málaga, opened by King Alfonso in 1926. You might be tempted by lunch, but ensure you have deep pockets if you consider staying the night.

St George's is better known as the Cementerio Inglés, the English Cemetery, the British Cemetery or the Protestant Cemetery and now features on many tourist maps of the city. It was created in the nineteenth century. Religious practice in Spain had been dominated by the Roman Catholic Church for

The entrance to the English Cemetery in Málaga. © Mike Shapton

hundreds of years. It was illegal for a non-Catholic to be buried in a Catholic cemetery. In Málaga, the authorities' preferred method of disposal was for the body to be buried upright in the sand of the beach. The waves and the local dogs would inevitably see to it that the corpse didn't stay there too long. Burial at sea was an alternative, and some people resorted to burying loved ones in a garden or orchard near their home. So in 1830 the then British Consul, William Mark, founded the cemetery as a final resting place for those who were not of the Roman Catholic faith. The cemetery is on a piece of rising ground, the earth dry and bare for much of the year. Consul Mark's own sepulchre can be found to the left of the path leading to the church of St George, where services are still held. The cemetery was the first of its kind to be created in Spain.[1]

Close to the small honey-coloured neoclassical church lies the grave of the man this book is about: George Langworthy.

1   R. Torres, *El cementerio de los Ingleses* (Ediciones Xorki, 2015) recounts the story of the cemetery and lists its 'occupants' and the stories of some of them. Not available in English

The inscription on the sepulchre of Consul William Mark. © Mike Shapton

The grave has been recently restored and the dedication reads 'Distingushed Benefactor and Adopted Favourite Son of the City of Torremolinos'. Next to his grave lies that of his wife, Annie Margaret 'the dearly loved wife of Major George Langworthy of Santa Clara, Torremolinos, who peacefully passed away 28 January 1913. One Faith One Hope One Spirit, In Him We Live United Still.' George survived his wife by over thirty-two years. The cemetery records give his date of death as 29 April 1945, although the restored grave bears the date 1946. Both Annie's and George's final journey will have taken them along the Paseo Reding from their home in Torremolinos, fifteen or so kilometres away. The walk along the Paseo was very familiar to George. He had been making the trip to Málaga on almost a weekly basis to visit his wife's grave, and to call on expatriate friends who lived in this wealthy part of the city, at least up until the outbreak of the Spanish Civil War in 1936. He had continued his cemetery visits almost until the end of his life when a broken hip confined him to his bed and led in due course to his death from pneumonia.

George and Annie's home in Torremolinos was called Santa

A view of the graves of George and Annie, with the chapel in the background. © Mike Shapton

Clara when they were both alive. Long before his death George became universally loved and respected by the local people, with the exception, perhaps, of the local Roman Catholic clergy and their more wealthy supporters for reasons that will become clear. It is said that all the people of Torremolinos and its surroundings turned out for his funeral which will have taken place little more than twenty-four hours after his death as was the custom in Spain then. The spring weather will have produced the usual abundance in the gardens of his home and there will have been no shortage of flowers to pay tribute to him on his final journey. Some thought that he was an English 'lor' (lord). Some thought he had married into the British royal family. Many thought he was no more nor less than a saint, not only for giving his money away to the poor, but for the way he conducted himself and treated everyone equally regardless of their social standing, for his steadfast religious belief and for his care and compassion. He could never imagine as a child growing up in a comfortable Manchester family that he would spend half his life, and end his days, in the warmth of the Spanish sun and the warmth of the people he had come to think of as his family.

CHAPTER TWO
Cottonopolis

The person whose loss was being mourned on that spring day in the south of Spain came into the world in the summer of 1865 in Manchester. By the time he was nine he was a wealthy little boy, one of the richer citizens of 'Cottonopolis', to give his home city the nickname it had acquired from being the centre of the Lancashire cotton industry. His father and his two uncles all had a hand in shaping his destiny though only one of them has left much of a mark behind him and that is one of George's uncles, Edward Ryley Langworthy.

The story of the Langworthy wealth begins in London where Edward Langworthy, a gentleman from Somerset and merchant in London, and his wife Sarah Ryley had their three sons, George, Edward Ryley and Lewis, all of whom would eventually make a living in Manchester. The first to arrive was George. We will call him 'George senior' to avoid confusion with our central character. George senior established the firm of George Langworthy & Co. in about 1822 and in 1834 the firm is listed in Pigot's Directory as a manufacturer of nankeens and bed-ticks at 113 Cannon Street. Langworthy Bros. & Co. Limited was established in 1840 when George senior was joined by his two brothers. By 1851 George senior is fifty-nine and married to his wife, Elizabeth, twenty-nine years his junior and has the first of his two children, a son, Edward Martin. His family will be completed by the arrival of his daughter in 1856. Edward Martin Langworthy also left his mark in history for very different reasons as we will discover later in this book.

While George senior led the way in establishing himself in Manchester, the youngest of the three brothers, Lewis, is spotted in 1833 in the passenger lists of the good ship *Roscoe* describing himself as a merchant and bound for New York. However, in Pigot and Slater's Directory of 1841 he is listed as a fustian and drill manufacturer. Lewis's contribution to our story is fundamental of course: he and his wife Hannah are the parents of young George and of considerably more Langworthy children. They had at least thirteen children, of whom most, but not all, survived into adulthood. That is quite an achievement for Victorian England, though their wealth will have been a key factor in this success. It is quite an achievement too that Hannah survived so many births. She was born Hannah Higinbottom Southam, the daughter of a coal merchant from Ashton under Lyne and was just eighteen when she married the thirty-nine-year-old Lewis. She had her first child eleven months later. George was the eleventh of the thirteen children, and the third of their four sons. Only two of his sisters outlived George: Christiana, born in 1856, and Ida, born 1864, who both died in 1949.

We will call the middle brother, Edward Ryley Langworthy, 'ERL' as he had a father and two nephews also bearing the name Edward. Merchant, politician and benefactor, ERL had no children of his own, which was to prove an important factor in the young George's destiny. ERL had married his wife Sarah Heaven in Gloucester in 1831 while working for C. Taylor and Sons & Co. of London as their representative in South America and Mexico. ERL shows on the electoral register for Rusholme in 1836, but one account has him still working as a foreign merchant. Whatever the precise detail, he must have amassed considerable capital and skill in managing investments. The firm of Langworthy Bros. & Co. was established in Greengate, Salford in 1840, most probably funded by ERL's capital. Greengate Mills has been described as one of the 'giants' of the local cotton mills. To gain an idea of the scale of the factory, the frontage on the River Irwell extended to over 200 metres.

At the same time ERL and Sarah had moved into a fine house in Victoria Park Crescent in Manchester. In 1846 he had Langdale built for him in Upper Park Road, Victoria Park.

Drawing of Greengate Mills. Courtesy of Ian Alistair Moss via Pinterest

When the house was offered for sale at the end of the nineteenth century the description ran:

> The house contains on the ground floor, vestibule, hall, drawing room, dining room, morning room, servants' hall, and good offices; on the first floor six principal bedrooms and dressing room; on the second floor seven bedrooms. There is a good and productive kitchen garden. The pleasure grounds are well shrubbed and planted. The stabling is excellent, with living rooms over coach house. The other outbuildings comprise conservatory, greenhouses, stoves etc. The site is freehold and free from chief rent and contains 12,290 sq yds, [approx. 3 acres].[1]

According to the census records between 1851 and 1891 between five and eight servants lived in the house, as well as the groom and his family living in the coach house. A gardener lived off the premises. The house servants would usually include a footman, a cook and at least three maids. In 1910 the house became a hall of residence of the University of Manchester, which it remains up to the present day.

The contrast with Salford could not have been greater. Greengate Mills stood on the western bank of the River Irwell, the river that divided Manchester from Salford. The Irwell rises on the moors of north Lancashire between Burnley and Bacup and flows more or less south, merging with the Mersey soon after its passage between Salford and Manchester. The river in the nineteenth century was described as a 'vile open sewer polluted not only by Salford itself but by the outpourings of some 159 towns and villages in the valley above'.[2]

---

1   The house description and the details of the will later in this chapter are from https://rusholmearchive.org/langdalethe-home-of-edward-langworthy

2   Details of nineteenth-century Salford and the direct quotations (apart from Engels) are from T. Bergin, D. N. Pearce, S. Shaw, *Salford: A City and Its Past* (City of Salford Cultural Services Department, 1975).

More vividly, the Scottish geologist Hugh Miller described it thus in 1862, three years before young George's birth:

> The hapless river . . . loses caste as it gets among the mills and the printworks. There are myriads of dirty things given it to wash, and whole wagon-loads of poisons from dye-houses and bleachyards thrown into it to carry away; steam-boilers discharge into it their seething contents and drains and sewers their fetid impurities till at length it rolls on – here between tall dingy walls, there under precipices of red sandstone, considerably less a river than a flood of liquid manure, in which all life dies whether animal or vegetable and which resembles nothing in nature except, perhaps the stream thrown out in eruption by some mud-volcano.

Salford itself, like its neighbour Manchester, expanded rapidly during the nineteenth century. R. L. Greenall recounts the diverse sources of this expanding population:

> Dalesmen from Cumberland and Westmorland, plainsmen from Cheshire, rural Lancastrians, pauper apprentices from the south, Scotsmen, Irishmen both Catholic and Protestant, German capitalists, Jews from the Rhineland, and later from Czarist Poland and Russia.

When Salford appointed its first Medical Officer of Health in 1868, it was one of the three or four unhealthiest places in Britain and death rates in the Greengate district where the Langworthys' mill was situated were very high. The principal killers were tuberculosis and other diseases of the lungs, bronchitis and infectious diseases like scarlet fever, typhoid and dysentery.

People like the three Langworthy brothers will have been well aware of all of this and of the poverty and squalor which accompanied it. They employed nearly a thousand operatives. Greengate Mills were described by the *Manchester Guardian* as 'on a very extensive scale, regarded as a model of arrangement and often visited by distinguished foreigners'. Mechanised cotton mills were, by modern standards, horrendous places to work. The noise was deafening so that workers used a form of lip-reading to communicate. The vast machines never ceased to turn, so cleaning and maintenance were carried out while they were in motion. Injuries such as loss of fingers and limbs were common, and even scalpings happened where girls' or women's hair was caught up in the machines. But they were a part of Britain's industrial revolution, and the brothers will have held the Victorian view that poverty was the result of personal failings rather than the more complex social structural explanations now accepted. They could have reasoned that they had succeeded through their own efforts, rather than inherited wealth like the landowners and others whose social status they were now emulating.

One person who took a different view was Karl Marx whose main benefactor, Friedrich Engels, was from a family involved in the Manchester cotton industry. In his seminal work, written between 1844 and 1845, *The Condition of the Working Class in England* and in the section of 'The Great Towns' Engels had this to say about Salford:

> If we cross the Irwell to Salford, we find, on a peninsula formed by the river, a town of eighty thousand inhabitants, which, properly speaking, is one large working man's quarter, penetrated by a single wide avenue. Salford, once more important than Manchester, was then the leading town of the surrounding district to which it still gives its name, Salford Hundred. Hence it is that an old and therefore very unwholesome, dirty, and ruinous locality is to be found here, lying opposite the Old Church of Manchester, and in as bad a condition as the Old Town on the other side of the Irwell.
>
> All Salford is built in courts or narrow lanes, so narrow that they remind me of the narrowest I have ever seen, the little lanes

of Genoa . . . The narrow side lanes and courts of Chapel Street,
Greengate and Gravel Lane have certainly never been cleansed
since they were built.[1]

While not sharing the analysis that Marx subsequently
presented, many Victorians felt it right to take action against
the extreme conditions that they witnessed, perhaps out of
self-interest and to prevent rather than foment revolution.
For example, in the 1860s medical charities were founded to
minister to those who had fallen ill from infectious disease in
their own homes. The aim was to prevent the infection of whole
families who would then be forced into the workhouse and be
'pauperised', effectively becoming a burden on the parish. It is
true, as well, that the era witnessed much activity which could
properly be considered altruistic. The first Medical Officer of
Health, Dr Syson, and his successors in Salford undertook a long
campaign to bring the facts of the situation to the attention of
the wider public and fight for the public health measures which
would begin to ameliorate the situation.

ERL clearly had some sense of civic responsibility. He had
become involved in politics soon after his arrival in the area.
When Salford was incorporated as a municipal borough in 1844,
ERL was elected as the first alderman for Trinity ward. He was
the borough's fifth mayor elected for two consecutive terms
from 1848 to 1850. In January 1857, Salford's Liberal MP Joseph
Brotherton died. ERL was selected as the party's candidate for
the vacancy, and as the only nominee, was elected to Parliament
unopposed on 2 February. Following his election he gave a
speech outlining his political views: he supported the temperance
movement, free trade and civil and religious freedom, the reform
of parliament and the strengthening of local government but he

1   F. Engels, *Condition of the Working Class in England* (Panther Edition,
1969), see https://www.marxists.org/archive/marx/works/download/pdf/condition-
working-class-england.pdf

opposed any increase in the size of the country's armed forces. He was only Salford's MP for a matter of months, as he did not stand at the subsequent general election later in the year.

Brotherton, who was fourteen years older than ERL, had been a member of a group which campaigned for parliamentary reform. This called for the redistribution of representation in the Houses of Parliament away from the rotten boroughs towards the fast-growing industrialised towns. The group's aims were achieved with the passing of the Reform Act 1832. Brotherton was elected as Salford's first MP at the ensuing General Election. He was re-elected five times, unopposed on two occasions. In parliament he campaigned against the death penalty, for the abolition of slavery and for free non-denominational education. It is likely that ERL held similar views, though it is ironic that men who advocated the abolition of slavery, which was enacted in Britain in 1833, should benefit so much from the cotton grown by slaves in the USA where it was not abolished until 1865 after the Civil War.

In terms of philanthropy, ERL's personal preference was to support what was often referred to as the 'betterment' of the working classes. In August 1846, a piece of land on the banks of the Irwell was opened as the Peel Park in honour of Sir Robert Peel, the son of a wealthy textile manufacturer from Bury who had subscribed to the public fund which had enabled the purchase of the land. The mansion house that already existed on the land opened as a free Museum and Library in 1849 mainly due to the efforts of Brotherton and to ERL who was, by then, mayor of Salford. The importance of this event was marked by the fact that Queen Victoria and Prince Albert became patrons and granted it the title 'The Royal Museum and Library', a name which was in use until 1940. On his death, ERL left £10,000 to the museum and library. A wing in the museum (the original building has since been demolished) was named after him and his portrait painted in 1853 by Philip

Westcott, is kept in the art gallery. ERL made similar bequests of £10,000 (about £850,000 in current values) to Manchester Grammar School for Boys for the establishment of twenty scholarships from the income of the bequest. His other, and most notable, bequest was another £10,000 to Owens College (which became the University of Manchester) to establish a

Ernest Rutherford with Hans Geiger in their lab in 1908.
Copyright of the University of Manchester.

professorship in experimental physics. His will stated the wish 'that students may be instructed in the method and experiment of research and that science may be advanced by original investigation.' Within one generation the Professorship had its first Nobel Laureate when Ernest Rutherford won the Nobel Prize in Chemistry in 1908. Four more Langworthy Professors won Nobel Prizes in Physics in subsequent years.[1]

1   Rutherford, a New Zealander, won the Nobel Prize in Chemistry in 1908 for work principally done at McGill University in Canada, but he had moved to Manchester in 1907. In 1919, Rutherford transformed nitrogen into oxygen, the

[Continued overleaf]

The wealth which supported this philanthropy and the family's prosperous lifestyle did not come solely from cotton. By the time that Manchester earned the nickname 'Cottonopolis' in about 1870, the city was not itself so much manufacturing cotton goods but was the centre of a web of cotton-making towns and was moving into its full prosperity as a financial and commercial centre. Because of this, Manchester itself escaped the worst effects of the 'cotton famine' of 1861–5 when overproduction and the interruption of cotton imports caused by the American Civil War caused widespread hardship in those towns.

Manchester was not the only provincial city to make money in the nineteenth century. Manchester, Leeds and Birmingham had emerged as industrial centres in the second half of the eighteenth century. All three were at the centre of a network of towns engaged in similar manufacturing: metalware in the Midlands, wool textiles in Yorkshire and cotton in Lancashire. The population growth between 1801 and 1851 was huge: Leeds went from 53,000 to 172,000. Birmingham from 75,000 to 247,000 and Manchester from 75,000 to 303,000, making them three of the most populous places in the country. The growth continued relentlessly during the second half of the century. By 1901 Manchester's population was 645,000, though a report from the Manchester Corporation in the 1880s cautioned that it was difficult to give an exact figure. This was because of

---

first successful transformation of one element into another, and in 1932, he was successful in splitting the atom for the first time. In 1915, William Lawrence Bragg became the youngest ever Nobel Laureate at twenty-five, winning the Nobel Prize for Physics alongside his father for 'services in the analysis of crystal structure by means of X-ray'. Patrick Maynard Stuart Blackett became the third holder of the Langworthy Professorship to win a Nobel Prize. His work looking at the tracks of atomic nuclear disintegration earned him the Nobel Prize for Physics in 1948. The next two winners both came in 2010, when Andre Geim and Konstantin Novoselov won the Nobel Prize for Physics for their ground-breaking discovery of graphene. Geim was the Langworthy Chair at the time of the Nobel Prize, with Novoselov taking over in 2013.

Hans Geiger was at Manchester from 1906 to 1912, his name is attached to several inventions, most notably the Geiger counter.

Primarily from www.manchester.ac.uk

the effects of suburbanisation, boundary changes and unchecked growth. In the second half of the century the three cities appeared to be more like provincial metropolises with only London, Liverpool and Glasgow boasting larger populations. The engineering and clothing trades were overtaking the original industries which were to be found in the 'satellite' towns. Grace's Guide for 1891 records 1,793 cotton mills in Lancashire, which between them contained 42,410,701 spindles and 610,934 looms.[1]

In Manchester itself, an increasing amount of business consisted of marketing and distribution, plus service industries such as banking and insurance. The Langworthy family were part of this shift. While still operating the mill they had founded in 1840 they were moving firmly into the merchant class and investing widely. Family members were involved in a variety of financial ventures including banking, railways and land acquisition. ERL himself retired from the family partnership in 1870 and in 1874 died from paralysis of the lungs. In his will he had a fortune of £1,200,000 to dispose of (about £100 million now). Apart from the bequests to Manchester Grammar School and the University of Manchester that I mentioned earlier, the bulk of the inheritance went to the family. His wife Sarah inherited the house and contents plus £300,000; the children of George senior (who had already died) received a total £150,000: the son, Edward Martin Langworthy, £100,000; the daughter Florence Honor Langworthy, £50,000 in trust; Lewis's sons including young George £35,000 each; Lewis's daughters and their children £25,000 in trust; Lewis £20,000; Hannah (Lewis's wife) for life and at her decease her children £10,000; a total of another £120,000 to various relatives, friends and servants.

So, at the age of nine, George inherited from his uncle £35,000, approximately £4 million at today's values.

1   Grace's Guide to British Industrial Industry, see https://www.gracesguide.co.uk/1891

CHAPTER THREE
Uppingham and Manliness

In May 1879 George was sent to board at Uppingham School in the county of Rutland. He may well have boarded at a preparatory school nearer home before this, but he was thirteen and three quarters years old when he arrived at Uppingham.

Uppingham is a small, pretty town in the smallest county in England, Rutland. In 1584 Robert Johnson, the Archdeacon of Leicester, founded a school there. Throughout the seventeenth,

Sketch of Uppingham from the southwest 1870. Published by John Hawthorn, courtesy Uppingham School

eighteenth and early nineteenth centuries the school catered for between thirty and sixty boys with two members of staff. Although it occasionally produced a pupil who achieved some distinction in later life, it hardly occupied a significant place in the English education landscape. All that was to change after the appointment of a new headmaster in 1853. The reason George ended up there in 1878 may also be connected to a singular event which happened in the years

Edward Thring mid 1860s.
Caltrop Album, courtesy of Uppingham School.

1875 and 1876 which brought added respect and fame to the school and its headmaster.

In 1853, the Revd Edward Thring successfully applied for the post of headmaster. He had no experience of running a school and had not even been to Uppingham. By the time of his death thirty-four years later, he had an international reputation as an innovator in education. Thring was strongly motivated by his own experience at a barbaric preparatory school followed by an equally harsh experience at Eton where there were only nine masters for 570 boys and the scholars were locked into a single room from 8.00 pm till 6.00 am the following morning with no adult supervision. The environment he aimed to create at Uppingham was in direct contrast to his experience at Eton. He believed that: boys should have some privacy; they should not be subjected to the will of the strongest or oldest; and every boy should get proper attention regardless of their level of ability. His approach to teaching had been further developed by a stint working with the children of the poor in Gloucester who presented him with a teaching challenge he would never have experienced amongst the young of the wealthy. Here he developed the axiom: 'The worse the material, the greater the skill of the worker'.

Thring was a small stocky man with wide-set penetrating blue eyes. At about the time that he became headmaster he also married his wife, a German by the name of Marie Koch who was accompanied by her sister Anna. Between them the women promoted a family atmosphere and established an efficient adminstraive regime, something that Thring was later to declare as essential to a good school. It was said that Thring's mood could always be read quite clearly on his face. The author E. W. Hornung, who was at the school with George, described Thring as 'majestic, noble and austere'.[1]

Thring came to Uppingham at a time when a rising middle class, people such as the Langworthys, were seeking good quality secondary education. Boarding schools in the late eighteenth and early nineteenth century had a reputation for violence and barbarism. Reform and improvement, most notably by Thomas Arnold at Rugby had led to the foundation in the 1840s of new schools at Cheltenham, Marlborough and elsewhere based on the model of Arnold's Rugby. When Gladstone opened Liverpool Collegiate College in 1843 he spoke of the need for new middle class secondary schools. This demand was matched by another important factor: railways. In 1848 and 1851, stations were opened at Manton (four miles from Uppingham) and Seaton (three miles from the town) respectively. This proved to be a critical factor in bringing the new middle classes to his school and Thring would personally greet new parents and boys at the station and urge

---

1   Ernest William Hornung (1866–1921) is best known for creating the character Raffles, a gentleman thief in late nineteenth-century London. Although his books are no longer popular, Raffles has featured in films and TV series. Hornung also wrote a novel based on his experience of Uppingham: *Fathers of Men* (1912). In 1893, Hornung married one of the sisters of Sir Arthur Conan Doyle, Constance ('Connie') Aimée Monica Doyle.

them to walk the three or four miles back to the school while the boy's luggage was loaded onto a trap.

The school went from strength to strength in the early years of Thring's tenure. By 1865 the number of boys was three hundred (it had been under fifty when he arrived) and the teaching staff of four had expanded to fourteen assistant masters and five staff teaching the 'extra' subjects. Comparisons were being made with the public schools of long standing such as Eton, Harrow, Winchester and Charterhouse. Two major challenges lay ahead in the years before George Langworthy was to arrive at the school. In the 1850s and 1860s four commissions were established to review and reform education. The fourth of these, the Taunton Commission affected Uppingham and between the years 1868 and 1873, Thring was engaged in battles on various fronts to defend and assert his model of education. The Commission had the power to impose a number of measures on a school like Uppingham that Thring opposed. It set him at odds with his governors and with some of his teaching staff. It was only when two parents stepped in for fear of Thring resigning that he began to get his way. His dealings with other headmasters about that time also led him to involvement in the founding of the Headmasters' Conference whose first ever meeting was held at Uppingham in 1869.

The fundamentals of Thring's educational philosophy have been summarised under the following four headings:

Every boy in the school must receive equal and full attention. This relates to the need for sufficient teaching staff to educate and supervise the pupils.

An ordinary boy should have as much time spent on him in the classroom as a brilliant boy. This remains a controversial view as some fear the less able hold back the most able and consequently the school's reputation. It contrasts with Arnold's view at Rugby to 'get rid of unpromising subjects'.

A boy not intellectually gifted should have opportunities to succeed in other occupations. Much education at the time was confined to the classics and mathematics, no doubt in part because they were the strengths of those who taught the children of the wealthy. Thring introduced 'extra' subjects including French, German, science, history, art, music and carpentry.

Machinery, machinery, machinery should be the motto of every good school. This means that a school needs an efficient system of

Uppingham's old school house, 1887. Anna Koch album, courtesy of Uppingham School

organisation backed by adequate buildings and equipment.

The second crisis of Thring's time at the school occurred in 1875. In June, a boy in the lower school died of typhoid fever. This was not in itself a remarkable event: five thousand people a year died of it in the whole of England at that time. The boys returned in September after their summer holiday, but within a month there were forty-six cases and four boys had died by the end of October, followed by a housemaster and his three-year-old son. Parents began to telegraph the school to send their sons home. The school was dispersed on 2 November and Thring spent the next few weeks having the school's drains put into good condition. The boys returned on 15 January but there was a new outbreak in February, though no deaths. This time the cause was identified as the town sewer which had not been cleaned out or repaired in the period when the school's drainage was receiving attention. Nevertheless, more telegrams arrived and the very existence of the school was under threat. Not only had Thring and his assistant schoolmasters invested their time, energy and talents into building the school up, but they had also invested money, and their income depended on the fees paid by the parents. After much deliberation, the decision was made to leave Uppingham until the threat of disease had been removed, and the chosen destination was Borth on the Welsh coast, north of Aberystwyth.

The anticipated stay of one term lengthened into a whole year because of delays to the sanitary work in Uppingham. The forced exile presented Thring and his staff with a unique challenge. The fact that only three boys did not follow the school to Wales must have been a source of great encouragement and demonstrated the parents' confidence. In addition it shattered a form of complacency which had begun to develop as a consequence of the school's improving reputation. The move revived the pioneering atmosphere which had motivated Thring's early years. Thring might have been tempted to consider the enforced move to be an Act of God. It had halted the school from following most of the other leading schools towards a culture dominated by athletic prowess, especially in team games like cricket and rugby. While at Borth the school could no longer compete against schools further away than Shrewsbury and did not have the pitches for many to play team games. Gymnastic activity, swimming and athletics regained their place alongside cricket in the school's physical education. Rambles along the shoreline and inland added a new dimension to the curriculum. When the school returned to Uppingham two years before George arrived, music, the classics and Christian worship had regained status in the list of school activities much to the delight of Thring and his belief that 'manliness was not just a matter of athletic prowess or military might'.

Although Thring had been headmaster of the school since 1853 and was now in his sixties, the Borth experience gave him a new lease of life. When they did return to Uppingham the townsfolk were glad of the renewed trade and employment opportunities that had been lost during their absence. At a national level, *The Times* newspaper invited Thring to write articles about the experience,

Cambrian Hotel yard and school room, Borth. Birley album, Borth Archive, courtesy of Uppingham School.

while congratulations came from other headmasters and from military men who admired his ability in organising such a complex operation. No doubt his wife and sister-in-law deserved much of the credit for this.

It was into this atmosphere that George Langworthy entered in May 1879. At that time, boys did not necessarily start at a new school at the beginning of the academic year (September), but because of Borth, Uppingham had abandoned the system of two long 'halves' to the year in favour of three terms a year beginning in January, April or May, and September. Why Uppingham was chosen for

George, and for his younger brother Edward, is not known. Neither of their older brothers had attended. It may relate to the school's increasing fame after Borth. Another reason may be that one of the trustees most supportive of Thring throughout the Borth experience and afterwards was a Mr T. H. Birley of Manchester, who may have been known to the Langworthys. In addition, in 1884 three bishops made speeches at a ceremony to mark the tercentenary of the original foundation of the school. The most enthusiastic of these was Bishop Fraser of Manchester.

Thring held strong views on the size of the school, which gradually increased under his headship and was probably near maximum when George joined. The maximum capacity would be 330; the optimum size for a class was twenty-three, and for a boarding house it was thirty-one. The boarding house where George Langworthy lived was called Old Constables and was built in 1860 on the site of the Horse and Trumpet Inn. On the 1881 census, when George was half way through his time at Uppingham, there were twenty-eight boarders in Old Constables, including himself, plus the housemaster, Alfred J. Tuck, his sister and cousin. George's younger brother Edward had recently joined the school and was boarded a few minutes' walk away on Stockerston Road. George's house was almost opposite the entrance to the school on the High Street. The census of 1881 which features George in his house lists boys from a wide variety of places across the country, including E. W. Hornung.

There is no detailed record at the school of each boy's individual achievements, including George's, but he did not represent the school in any sports and he was not a 'praepostor' (prefect). If he was not a particularly gifted pupil then Thring's educational philosophy would have stood him in good stead. It is surprising that he did not represent the school at sport considering the abilities he later showed as a cavalry officer, but it is possible that he excelled at a sport which was played at Uppingham, and which, incidentally, Thring loved and that is fives. Fives is an English sport in which a ball is propelled against the walls of

Old Constables, 1862. Constables Archive, courtesy of Uppingham School

a three or four-sided special court using a gloved or bare hand.
Other sports are played on similar walled courts ranging from
squash to Basque 'pelota'. There are two main types of fives:
Rugby Fives and Eton Fives. Rugby Fives is played in a four-
walled court similar to a squash court and the ball is harder than
the one used in Eton Fives, Eton Fives was the variety played at
Uppingham in a court enclosed on three sides and open at the
back. The ball is slightly lighter and softer and the glove worn is
thin. It is played as a doubles game and the court contains some
'hazards'. These include a step splitting the court into upper and
lower sections and a buttress protruding into the court in line

with the step. The reason for these hazards is that the game was played in the bays between the buttresses of the chapel at Eton College and the bay at the foot of the chapel steps had additional hazards on which the Eton style court is based. The game was played at Eton when Thring was there and where he developed his love of it. The game is alive and well and the modern Eton Fives Association has thirty-five member clubs, based mainly on

A game of fives. Courtesy of Eton Fives Association

public schools and Oxbridge. At Uppingham in George's day, Old Constables had its own fives court, and the speed and agility required in the game may have appealed to George more than the cricket field.

There is another aspect of Thring's approach which may have stayed with George throughout his adult life, and that is Thring's view of how a life should be lived, which led to his constant repetition of the phrase 'true life'. It could be summed up as self-denial, patience, love, courage and steadiness, but comes from an

The original fives court at Eton College. Courtesy of Eton Fives Association

unfolding philosophy popular in Christian thinking in Victorian times drawing on Plato. Plato believed in the ideal of beauty and goodness and Thring believed that the role of education was to draw out the inherent beauty and goodness of his pupils. At the time the more popular method seemed to be to beat knowledge into unwilling, unpleasant scholars.

Thring would explain:

> Plato believed there were three elements to a man's soul. One of them, our basic needs, for food, for warmth, etc, does not require education. The second element, the spirited, is the source of courage and self-confidence, which is realised in ambition and self-assertiveness. The third element, the rational or philosophical, embraces the pursuit of intellect and all learning.

Thring believed that there must be a balance of all three elements to produce the whole man, who should aspire to three virtues: truth, courage and self-control which Thring encapsulated into the concept of 'manliness'. This was not a concept of aggressive masculinity, a fantasy warrior status. True manliness, Thring argued, aimed to produce the balanced all-rounder, the whole man, 'the gentle, very perfect knight' –loyal to his king and to his God, bound to defend the weak, succour the oppressed and put down the wrong-doer. This contrasted with the muscular Christian manliness which had found favour in other public schools. Neither intellectual strength nor bodily strength was to be praised at Uppingham; more a Platonic harmony of body, intellect and soul. This concept lay behind his determination to offer a curriculum much wider them most public schools at the time so that boys could excel in a number of ways. Another consequence of the philosophy was to give boys a degree of freedom which was unusual in equivalent schools. The purpose of this was to enable them to develop and test the virtues Thring espoused. Boys were given a degree of trust but in return the boys were expected to trust the staff. With trust comes freedom, Thring argued, and with freedom responsibility for oneself, for one's actions. He would warn pupils that a breach of trust or an abdication of responsibility would have severe consequences.

Given how the second half of George Langworthy's life turned out, perhaps this teaching lodged somewhere in his memory.

Four years after George left the school, Thring, already a committed member of the Headmasters' Conference, hosted the annual conference of the London Society of Schoolmistresses which, despite its name was a national organisation of women involved in the higher education of girls. Thring advocated improving educational opportunities for girls and continued his support until his retirement. One comment after the event, which seemed to capture the view of the women was: 'No school has ever impressed me like Uppingham; other schools may be bodies corporate, but Uppingham has a *soul*'.

The Uppingham school day in Thring's time

6.00 am	School bell rang: also at 6.30 and 6.55 am. The boys then walked to the Schoolroom.
7.00 am	Schoolroom door shut. Prayers and roll call.
7.00–8.30 am	'First School', i.e. lesson: Latin prose or repetition.
9.00–10.00 am	Breakfast
10.00 am–12.00 pm	'Second School'. Other subjects, including English, history, etc.
12.00–1.30 pm	'Third School', mathematics and optional subjects like languages, chemistry, drawing and music.
1.30–2.30 pm	Lunch.
2.30–4.00 pm	Afternoon school on non-half holidays (4.00–5.25 pm in winter.
4.00–7.00 pm	Time for recreation and tea.
7.00–8.45 pm	(Except Saturday). The boys were required to be in their studies until prayers. Between 7.45 and 8.45 pm Thring made his round of the studies.
After prayers	There was three-quarters of an hour during which boys could visit the tuck shop in School Lane.

Uppingham School 'Dateline' by J. Rudman courtesy of Uppingham School.

The Headmistresses' Conference, 11 June 1887. Thring is stood in the centre. Green Cloth Album, courtesy Uppingham School.

CHAPTER FOUR
Horses, Hounds and Fusiliers

George left Uppingham in April 1883, just four months before his eighteenth birthday, and the only indications of where he went or what he did in the following four years are these items:

An announcement in the *London Gazette* in August 1885 that, 'George Langworthy, Gent.' was to become a lieutenant in 3rd Battalion, Lancashire Fusiliers.

An announcement of the results of the military competitive examination of lieutenants of militia for commissions in the line posted in the *London Gazette* of 4 May 1887, stating that George would join the 7th Dragoon Guards as a second lieutenant, alongside C. W. Battine of the 3rd Battalion Welsh Fusiliers.

There is also a record that a George Langworthy applied for a passport in July 1884.

By now, many family members had left the Manchester area, though two sisters were married and raising young families in the area. It is reasonable to assume from him joining the local militia that George may have returned to Manchester and used it at least as a base for living a full and active life as a wealthy young man. Although he would not come into his inheritance until he was twenty-one, the trustees of his inheritance will probably have responded favourably to any request to increase the allowance which would have maintained him at Uppingham. It was quite common in the era of railways and steam ships for wealthy

Victorians to travel and George may have made his first forays abroad after obtaining a passport.

The invention of the steam engine was perhaps the greatest single factor in transforming British society in the nineteenth century. If he did obtain his passport in 1884, perhaps he was venturing overseas by ship. By the 1880s steamships were large, powerful and efficient and routes had been opened up around the world. Perhaps his cousin, Edward Martin Langworthy, the subject of the next chapter, invited him to sail on his 235-ton steam yacht *Meteor*. On land, the steam engine had transformed travel. After the opening of the first inter-city railway in 1830 between Manchester and Liverpool, the network of lines had grown rapidly. By the 1880s a well established network enabled fast and comfortable travel to almost any part of the British mainland. While the canals had greatly improved the transport of bulky and heavy goods at slow speed, the train had totally eclipsed the horse as the means of flexible long distance travel.

He would not have been held back from travelling by his decision to become a lieutenant in the Lancashire Fusiliers. The 3rd and 4th Battalions were militia, that is to say part-time battalions and George's duties were unlikely to be too onerous. However, a commission in the militia was an alternative route to a regular army commission instead of going through the Royal Military College at Sandhurst. By this means, in 1887 George was to obtain his commission in the 7th Dragoon Guards.

George came from a family with no military background. None of his brothers nor his cousin followed a military career, but four years after leaving school, George was a second lieutenant in an élite cavalry regiment. The horse must have been a significant party of George's story in these four years. He would not have had any chance of riding at Uppingham, though during holidays he may well have visited and stayed with friends who rode, or even had fathers or uncles in cavalry regiments. Horse-racing and hunting on horses were both popular pastimes and George will have had the means to indulge in both, perhaps owning his first horses in this period. Several hunts operated in the countryside of Lancashire, Cheshire and Derbyshire surrounding Manchester.

Accepting that blood sports are not to most modern tastes, at the time they presented an opportunity of exhilarating, fairly dangerous competitive action, much in the same way as motor-racing opened up similar opportunities in the twentieth century. One of the ways in which cavalry regiments maintained their horsemanship wherever they were stationed was through hunting, so developing hunting skills before he became an officer would have stood George in good stead. It was, of course, a sport for the wealthy. Horses had to be bought, stabled and cared for. The right clothing and other accessories had to be just right. There was social life too; not just the socialising during a hunt itself, but hunt balls and other grand occasions.

One of the most fashionable hunts at the time was the Lyme Harriers. The Lyme estate sits south-east of Manchester and Stockport and had been in the Legh family since 1398. In the 1880s William John Legh, 1st Lord Newton was the owner. His investments included railways and he had a station built close to the estate in the village of Disley when he invested in the Stockport, Disley and Whaley Bridge Railway which now forms part of the Manchester to Buxton line. This ensured easy access from the nearby towns and cities. It might be the hunt George chose though no information exists. It was the hunt chosen by Friedrich Engels, Karl Marx's benefactor.[1]

Lyme and its estate lie just inside the Western Moorlands part of what is now the Peak District National Park. The land around Lyme rises a thousand feet from the Cheshire plain to the west. If George joined this hunt, he will have noticed that it undulates like the land around Uppingham, but here it was not put to crops

---

1 Professor Gunn (*see bibliography*) informed me verbally that Friedrich Engels was a member of the Lyme Harriers. The estate is now in the hands of the National Trust, who told me that no records of the hunt are at Lyme.

but was open moorland with scattered copses. Where boundaries needed to be marked, dry stone walls served where hedges and fences would feature in farmland. It was land that would have provided excellent territory for a young man keen to develop his horse-riding skills. There was ample stabling attached to the house at Lyme and George may well have been able to buy one or two horses and stable them there. Herds of red deer roam the estate now but in George's day they will also have been used as prey for the hunt with dogs. The word 'harrier' is defined as a hunter of hares so it may be that George will also have had experience of galloping across moorland in pursuit of these creatures too.

Horse-racing was another arena in which sport and socialising came together. The Legh family owned the race-course at Haydock Park in south-west Lancashire. George may well have visited the races here as well as other well-known courses such as Aintree where the Grand National was already an established fixture. 'Salford lads, Manchester men, Liverpool gentlemen' is a nineteenth century phrase which suggest Salfordians did the work, Mancunians built the enterprises and Liverpudlians made the deals, i.e. were merchants, dealing in all manner of commodities and more prone to gamble, where Manchester men were perhaps more puritanical, building wealth on enterprise and endeavour. Liverpool men were then more drawn to horse-racing and the attendant gambling, and by the 1880s Manchester was more a merchant city than a manufacturing one, all that having been 'outsourced' to the surrounding towns. Of course, these are middle class demarcations: the aristocracy would not have had reservations about enjoying any equine sports. George, then, would have felt quite at home on the turf even if his mother and aunts might not have approved. In George's later life as a cavalry officer, attendance at fashionable race meetings such as Ascot was in fact routine amongst regiments who were stationed at home.

Race meetings had also become an excellent place for encountering fashionable women. From 1878 onwards the Prince

of Wales (later to be King Edward VII) was a regular attender at
Aintree and in 1881 the Empress Elizabeth of Austria-Hungary
was at the Grand National which may have encouraged more
women to attend.

The hunt and the racecourse were not the only places where a
young man with money may take his pleasure. In the nineteenth
century Manchester Leeds and Birmingham 'were centres of
considerable cultural dynamism and innovation in their own
right, independent and in some respects in advance of London.'
The available opportunities ranged from the 'high' culture of
exclusive classical concerts to the 'low' culture of the music hall, and
gentlemen's clubs ranging from the conservative to the bohemian.

If racecourses were an opportune venue for admiring
fashionable women in their finery, gentlemen's clubs were
explicitly designed as places to exclude women. The nineteenth
century saw a proliferation of clubs in cities as the middle
classes expanded, benefitting from the fruits of the industrial
revolution. Manchester's Union Club, established in 1825 was
an example of an institution seeking to attract the wealthy
regardless of political or religious persuasion, with prominent
Liberals and Tories alike paying the entrance fee of 30 guineas
and the annual subscription of 5 guineas in the 1830s. This club
was still thriving in the 1880s but many more were flourishing,
catering for a variety of interests and tastes. The size and cost of
the clubs expanded as the century progressed. The new Reform
Club opened in Manchester in 1871 at a cost of £60,000 and the
Conservative Club in 1876 at a cost of £110,000 (£100,000 in 1875
is the equivalent of over £11 million today). By 1885, when George
was a young man of twenty in Manchester, the Conservative
Club (1,100 members) 'was staffed by "three tribes" of servants,
pages, liveried footmen and black-coated waiters, while the
Reform Club, with over two thousand members, employed sixty-
five staff by the early twentieth century.'

While the clubs were intentionally exclusive and private

other more public forms of entertainment were on offer but still affected by various forms of social and critical approval or disapproval. Hallé classical music concerts were regarded as the height of cultural achievement in the city from the late 1860s. Promenade concerts, introduced in 1871 widened access but were judged inferior. Theatre was emerging from the shadow of strong social disapproval but music hall continued to be condemned by the 'respectable' classes for its vulgarity and commercialism. It is possible that a young man such as George, freed of parental or scholarly oversight was as likely to be found in the auditorium of a music hall on occasion as much as in the audience of a Hallé concert at the Free Trade Hall. The city centre was used by 'the "gilded youth" of both sexes as a focus for courtship, consumption and fashionable display'.

Attendance at a Hallé concert was a 'highly visible ritual performance'. Ritual public performances, to display order and authority, were a frequent feature of Victorian cities and George, by becoming a lieutenant in the Lancashire Fusiliers, will have inevitably been part of that. He may well have participated in, or at least witnessed, grand processions as a child, given that his uncle had been a prominent civic leader. The northern city centres had been remodelled with noble, monumental buildings, and these formed a stage on which the successful could display themselves and their achievements. Early major performances had been to mark such events as the visit of the young Queen Victoria, but they became an institutionalised part of civic life. Inevitably the military were involved in such parades, but even though George was an officer in just a militia regiment, his formal uniform included a scarlet tunic and a bearskin. It may well be that he looked on with envy when cavalry formed a part of such processions.

The year before George joined the 7th, he attained the age of majority, then twenty-one, and it seems timely to review the Langworthy family before he sets off on the career that would take

The Langworthy Family Tree

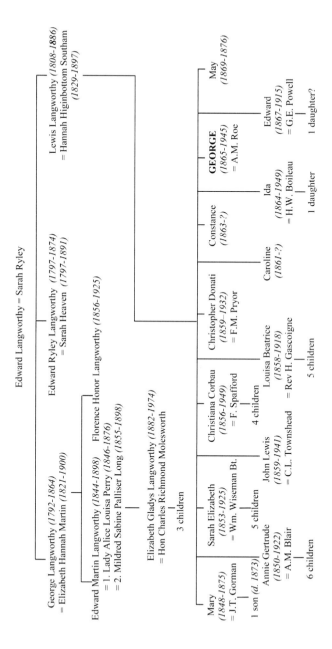

him to India and Egypt, South Africa, and then a life in Spain. The family name is uncommon and the first names quite varied, so publicly available documents give a fairly comprehensive picture of the family.

In 1886 George's father Lewis (b. 1808) had died. Although his home was by then in Surrey, he was buried back in Manchester. He was the last of the original 'Langworthy Bros.' to pass away. George (b. 1792) had died in 1864 and ERL (b. 1797) had followed in 1874.

Of the three widows, ERL's Sarah (née Heaven, b. 1797) remained in Manchester in the home she shared with him up until her death in 1891. The house subsequently became a women's hall of residence for the University of Manchester: Langdale Hall.

George's widow, Elizabeth Hannah (née Martin, b. 1821) had moved to Gay's House, Holyport near Maidenhead, Buckinghamshire, where she remained until her death in 1900. This house was even grander than ERL's in Manchester. A sale catalogue for its auction in 1931 (no Langworthy owned it then) described it as chiefly of the Queen Anne period with halls, four reception rooms, ten principal bedrooms plus five for servants, six bathrooms, a lodge, a 'farmery' of twenty-one acres, etc, the whole estate consisting of seventy acres. Her only daughter, Florence Honor Langworthy, lived with her and never married, dying at Gay's House in 1925. George and Elizabeth's only son was difficult to find in 1886 for reasons that will become apparent in the next chapter.

Lewis's widow, Hannah Higinbottom (née Southam, b. 1829) appears to have taken up residence with one of her daughters, Sarah, before Lewis's death. In the 1891 census she was living in Worcestershire and was still resident there on her death in 1897, though she died in St Vaucluse, France.

The situation of George's brothers and sisters was as follows:

Mary (b. 1848) had died in 1875, having married in 1870 and lost her only son in 1872 at the age of one.

Annie Gertrude (b. 1850) married Arthur McDonald Blair, a Manchester solicitor, in 1871. The 1881 census shows they had five children and another little one appears on the 1891 census alongside their five servants in Pendleton, Salford. She was to die in 1922.

Sarah Elizabeth (b. 1853) has married William, 9th Baronet Wiseman and was living in Essex with four children, her mother and four servants. A fifth child will arrive in 1890. Her husband died in 1893. She lived until 1925, her last address being in Putney.

John Lewis (b. 1854) married his wife Caroline in 1880. He lived in Dorking, Surrey, then in Hampshire and later in Devon. He married again in 1915 and died in Bath in 1941, four years before George.

Christiana Corbau (b. 1856) married a local solicitor, Frederick Spafford, in 1876 and was living in Altrincham, Cheshire with their four children and four servants. She died in Canterbury in 1949 at the age of ninety-three, the last surviving of George's siblings

Louisa Beatrice (b. 1858) attended school in Hampstead, London and later married the Revd Herbert Gascoigne. They had two children by 1886 and would go on to have another three. She died in Sussex in 1918. Herbert died in Buckinghamshire in 1936 aged eighty-two.

Christopher Donati (b. 1859) moved to Richmond in Surrey. In 1895 he married Florence Mary Pryor. He died in 1932.

Caroline (b. 1861) appears in the 1881 census at what may be a boarding school in Putney. No further information could be located.

Constance (b. 1863). In 1881 she is at the same address in Putney as Caroline. A woman of that name married in 1882 when Constance would have been nineteen, but no further information could be located.

Ida (b. 1864) married Henry Willock Boileau in St Paul's Cathedral, Calcutta on 26 Dec 1890. George's regiment was still in India at the time so it is reasonable to assume that he attended. They had one daughter, Mildred. Ida outlived George and, like Christiana, died in 1949. She is buried in Oxford with her daughter. Her husband appears to have settled in Bray, near to where Florence Honor Langworthy lived. He was a keen huntsman, glorying in the nickname 'Dog Face'.

George (b. 1865), we assume, is living in Manchester doing a bit of soldiering in his militia regiment and a lot of hunting. He may have been in residence with one of his married sisters as it was not common for young men to take rooms of their own in Manchester at the time. The extensive Victorian railway system would have made it easy to visit his spread out family if he wished.

Edward (b. 1867) attended Uppingham, like George, and went on to study law at Oxford. He had rooms in Knightsbridge, London and in 1898 married Gertrude Edith Powell and died in 1915 in Buenos Aires. Their one daughter did not bear his name: Corisande Winifred Yolande Powell (1904–2001)

May (b. 1869), the youngest, died in 1876.

CHAPTER FIVE
A Family Scandal

There are three Edward Langworthys in the two generations: George's uncle, Edward Ryley Langworthy (ERL), George's cousin Edward Martin Langworthy, who I will call EML for the sake of brevity and clarity, and George's younger brother Edward. ERL was regarded as a pillar of society in the Manchester region: successful businessman, public benefactor, mayor. His short spell as a member of parliament for Salford will not have made him a national reputation. The national reputation came to EML but not for such noble reasons. As one correspondent to the *Pall Mall Gazette* wrote, if 'one-fourth of the charges laid at the door of Edward Martin Langworthy be true, the man is proved to be as black a scoundrel as ever broke bread'. All following quotations in the text are from editions of the *Pall Mall Gazette* in April and May 1887.

The man who was responsible for EML's behaviour becoming so well known the length and breadth of the land, and beyond, goes by the name of William Thomas Stead. A man who earned the nickname 'Muckraker', he has been called the father of the modern tabloid newspaper. He is the subject of a recent biography by W. Sydney Robinson. After learning his trade on provincial papers, Stead became deputy editor of the *Pall Mall Gazette* in 1880, becoming editor in November 1883 when his predecessor resigned to become MP for Newcastle. Stead combined a devout

Christianity and strict moral sense with a desire to expose the evils and iniquities of Victorian society. To do so he employed journalistic sensationalism.

So it was that a certain Mrs Langworthy, formerly Miss Mildred Sabine Palliser Long entered the *Gazette's* offices and the tale she had to tell was recounted in the pages of the *Gazette* day after day, week after week, in 1887 and then reprinted by the newspaper in a stand-alone, best-selling 'extra'. Not surprisingly, the story was picked up in the regional press throughout the country and even appeared in papers as far afield as New Zealand's *Auckland Star* and *La Nación* in Buenos Aires. It is even said that EML was hissed off the platform at Santa Fe railway station by an indignant mob.

The story lived on. It was recounted in a book of gossip called *Further Indiscretions* published by a Mrs Stuart Menzies in 1918, picked up by a modern American writer of historical romances and even repeated in 2015 in *El Litoral* of Santa Fe, Argentina, which was where EML had his estates.

Under the title 'Strange But True Stories of Today', Stead gave the background plus a running commentary of legal developments. Calling him a 'Nabob of the Argentine', but describing him as 'plebeian in birth', Stead began by explaining how EML inherited from both his father and his uncle (ERL) and was, by 1883:

> Permanently resident at Bella Vista, a stately pleasure house which he has built for himself in the midst of his princely domain in the Argentine republic . . . the Langworthy Grant covers thirty-two square leagues in the north of Toscas . . . This however is only one of his estates. The estate of Curamalan on which Bella Vista stands, is about 70,000 acres in extent. In addition to this there is another estate in Paraguay . . . he owns 1,000 horses, 2,000 cows and 10,000 sheep.[1]

1 Details of the extent of EML's estates are confirmed in M. G. & E. T

[*Continued overleaf*]

At the time when he met Miss Long, he was in Europe, spending most of his time in his steam yacht *Meteor*, a floating palace of 235 tons, said to have cost him £9,000.

Stead now turns to 'a sweet girl graduate': 'Mildred Sabine Palliser Langworthy, the heroine of this tale is a lady by birth and education.' She studied for examinations at the University of Dublin and later at Cambridge, but soon after her father lost most of his money 'and from that day until her unfortunate marriage to Edward Langworthy the independent, high-spirited girl never cost her parents another sixpence'. She found work in Chiswick as a teacher and further successful appointments followed. Then in late in 1880 she fell and broke her arm and in February 1881 went with her brother to stay in the Hotel Bedford in Paris where she first met EML. 'He was very kind. She was very interesting with her pale face and her bandaged arm.' They met again in September when she declined his invitations but the following summer (1882) he called on her frequently in London and she accepted an invitation to the theatre.

> After going to the theatre it was but a step to visiting the yacht . . . Returning to town . . . he accompanied her home . . . he exclaimed, 'You don't know how pretty you are,' and, kissing her, passionately asked her to be his wife. She consented. There is no need to linger over the scene . . . And so the brief visit ended in a plighted troth, and thus it came to pass that Mildred Long was engaged to Edward Langworthy.

EML would not let Mildred meet his mother and claimed she disapproved of the engagement, but he managed to persuade

---

Mulhall, *Handbook of the River Plate* (Kegan, Paul, Trench & Co., 6th ed., 1892).

EML founded a colony, named Florencia (after his sister?) in 1885 and sold it three years later to a joint stock company, perhaps to support his assertion in the British courts that he had no significant assets.

Mildred not to break it off and, what's more, to visit his yacht
with a chaperone. The *Meteor* was lying at Dartmouth. 'The
crew consisted of sixteen men all told. As Mr Langworthy was
fond of shooting, he travelled with gamekeeper and dogs.' EML
introduced her to respectable friends at Dartmouth as he also
did at Cherbourg after he persuaded her they should go there.
After leaving her on the yacht for a day he urged her to visit Caen
with him, leaving the chaperone behind. After they had visited
the cathedral he directed the carriage into the countryside and
declared that they were to be married.

> Miss Long was startled. The sudden announcement almost took
> away her breath. She could only stammer, 'But will it be right?'
> 'Right?' he replied enthusiastically. 'Of course it will be right. I
> cannot bear long engagements. Don't be cross darling but we are to
> be married this very day: all is arranged.'

Stead acknowledges her behaviour is unwise, but manages to
excuse it.

> The carriage stopped . . . at . . . a Catholic church some miles in
> the country from Caen . . . The priest, a greasy looking cleric with
> sharp black eyes and a somewhat insolent smile . . . went through
> some service . . . At its close, Mr Langworthy turned to her and
> exclaimed, 'Now I've secured my darling, and you cannot run away
> from your Bear (a pet name of his) any more.' 'But don't we sign
> our names to anything?' she asked. 'No,' said he. He paid the priest
> 400 francs and all was over.

Not surprisingly, Mildred had severe doubts. They argued.
Promises were made and broken. Nevertheless, she spent months
with him on the yacht and he finally arranged a second ceremony
to take place in Antwerp.

The Revd Dr. Potts, an elderly divine, was duly ordained to the
ministry of the Presbyterian Church of America . . . When the
first application was made to him to make two lovers man and
wife he hesitated and consulted a member of his committee . . .
[and concluded] . . . that he was legally authorized to marry any
foreigners by the Presbyterian service provided they were English-
speaking people. Such was the gist of the evidence which he gave
afterwards before the special examiner of the High Court of Justice
on March 16, 1885, and no one ever imputed to him any intention to
act other than in good faith.

Stead argues that EML, as a barrister, would have known
that, to be legal, marriages in Belgium had to be ratified by the
civil authorities. Stead now indulges in one of his moral diatribes
against EML.

Whatever may be thought of the ethics of sexual relationship, there
is one point that even the most cynical debauchee admits to be
indefensible. To ruin a young life, to betray maiden innocence, to
triumph in the destruction of a woman's honour – that according
to the ethics of the man of the world is but a venial offence. But
when to seduction there is added hypocrisy, when the voluptuary
lulls the conscience of his victim to sleep by the sound of prayers
and holy words and when the cruellest wrongs which one human
being can do to another is accomplished by fraud, cloaked beneath
the form of religion, that is a crime which, even in the easy-going
ethics of society there is neither palliation nor excuse. It was this
crime of which Mr Edward Martin Langworthy was guilty at No
20, Avenue Rubens on January 10, 1883.

When the ceremony was over, Dr Potts made an entry in
his private register book and issued a marriage certificate which
he handed to Mildred. EML took it from her saying he would
deposit it for safe-keeping with his solicitors and made her swear

she would not mention the marriage for a year for fear he would be disinherited of his mother's fortune. In fact, a letter exists in which the then Lord Fitzsimmons of the Foreign Office was asked to inquire, on behalf of EML's mother, of the British consul in Antwerp if the ceremony had happened, though some of the facts offered do not tally with Stead's account which will have come from the lips of Mildred.

Days later, EML got everything ready for a voyage to end ultimately in Buenos Aires. Mildred's family were still unhappy with the relationship but she sailed with him. A cousin of his (most likely George's younger brother, Edward), and Edith, a sister of Mildred, accompanied them all the way to South America. They spent some weeks in Lisbon where Mildred told EML she was pregnant. He was not pleased and seems to have tried everything to induce a miscarriage: 'everything was done that a malignant ingenuity could devise in the way of alternate starving and feeding on unwholesome food, to produce violent sickness and extreme exhaustion'. EML even dosed her with morphia and mercury. Once the maid he employed, who obviously would follow his instructions, said, 'I don't know what you're made of, madame. That would have settled the business in any three other women.'

One night, Stead dubs it 'A Midnight Scene On Board the *Meteor*', Mildred decided to have it out with her husband.

> 'You've ruined me!' he cried. His wife, in a frenzy, rushed up the stairs out of the saloon upon the deck. It was eleven o'clock, the rain was falling in torrents, but she did not heed it. Her brain was on fire, her heart was cold as death. 'If I could but die,' she moaned. She was thinly clad in a low-necked, black-net evening dress. The rain soaked her through and through but she sat in silent agony, hour after hour, while the slow stars, faintly visible though the clouds, crawled across the pitiless sky and at last faded out of sight in the dawning day.

Although Stead had genuinely high moral standards and a strong Christian faith, his biographer Robinson says he was not immune to the charms of beautiful women and he suggests that for him Mildred epitomised female perfection and that he may have fallen in love with her. His style of journalism and his infatuation will have combined well to write passages like the one above.

EML duly continues in the role of villain, telling her the marriage was all a sham and repeating this to her sister. Now they were at Buenos Aires. Mildred and her sister were not allowed to land and the same evening they were taken down river to a ship that was to return them to Europe. EML had given her 'tickets made out in a false name, a sum of £50, a box of baby clothes and a letter'. The ship that awaited them was not the Royal Mail steamer they expected but 'a dirty miserable French ship which had lost its deckhouse on the last voyage and was still undergoing repair'.

> It was a squalid doghole of a cabin where they found themselves, but they were far better off than on board Mr Langworthy's floating palace. For the captain was a humane man. He nursed Mrs Langworthy with the tenderness of a woman, and on the sixth day she had recovered sufficiently to leave her berth. She crept to her box, where Mr Langworthy had told her she would find the baby clothes for her child – and his. She opened it. All that was inside was ten yards of coarse white calico and six yards of red flannel.
>
> When she saw that, for the first time her love for her husband wavered and fled. As she simply says: 'Then I hated Mr Langworthy.'

Mildred returned to her father and after the birth of the baby, a girl, she began proceedings against EML and so began a long game of cat and mouse, both verbal and physical. Mildred had finally found a firm of solicitors, Lumley and Lumley, who would take up her case to establish that she was EML's wife and that therefore she was entitled to alimony. EML was represented by Messrs Bircham. EML consistently claimed that he was in Argentina though it emerged in an affidavit that he had been interviewed in England, an interview in which he emphatically denied that any marriage had taken place between him and Mildred. On the strength of this and other affidavits Mildred's claim for alimony was ruled out by the courts. Then, early in 1885, Dr Potts, the American Presbyterian minister who had performed the ceremony in Antwerp happened to come to London and gave evidence that the ceremony did take place and his evidence was supported by a witness to the ceremony. Having consistently denied any ceremony had taken place, EML's solicitors now changed tack, admitting everything, but questioning the legality of the marriage. They did this just at the point when Mildred would have been able to step into a witness box and tell her story in open court.

In their telling of the story, the *Pall Mall Gazette's* anger was now directed at EML's solicitors as much as at EML. Letters sent by Messrs Bircham to the *Gazette* were published in the *Gazette* and responded to in its columns. The *Gazette* had now been running the story on a daily basis for just under two weeks and on 29 April 1887 they included a summary of events from the couple's first meeting in February 1881, through to alimony of £1,200 per annum being granted in 1886, to the case going to the Court of Appeal in March 1887 where EML sought a decree absolute of divorce. This was refused as he was not paying alimony or maintenance for the child. Meanwhile in 1886, Mildred had discovered that EML was in England buying goods and equipment to ship to Argentina and she also discovered the ship that they were due to be loaded onto. On her instruction, a 'posse of sheriff's officers' went to the dock to seize EML's goods. The goods included 'hampers of china, gun cases, boxes of ammunition, boxes of boots and shoes and men's wearing apparel and a great heap of other goods . . . there

were three cases, with ten ducks in all . . . two loads of hay and
a case of four swans . . . Then three heifers and a bull arrived.'
Meanwhile, EML's servants had tipped him and his mother off.
Mrs Langworthy Senior telegraphed that all the goods were hers,
and EML telegraphed to the ship to meet him at Lisbon. The
sheriff's men then felt unable to take possession of the goods.
Mrs Langworthy Senior bought all the goods off the sheriff's
men and sent them to Buenos Aires by the next boat and EML
returned to Argentina on another ship. Efforts to declare EML
bankrupt had been frustrated and that 'with intent to defeat or
delay his creditors, the said Edward Martin Langworthy on or
about the seventh day of April [1886] departed out of England'.
After efforts to delay the bankruptcy proceedings against him,
EML was declared bankrupt on 18 March 1887. EML appealed of
course, but lost his appeal.

At this point, Stead decided to comment on the behaviour of
what he called the 'Langworthy Clan', notably EML's aunt, the
widow of ERL (Edward Ryley Langworthy) who, we know from
Chapter Two, was very wealthy. Stead was clearly not impressed
by her summary refusal to have anything to do with the case
considering her philanthropic reputation in Manchester.

Meanwhile, from April 1887, readers of the *Gazette* were
beginning to send in donations to a fund to support her as she had
not received a penny of the alimony she was awarded in February
1886 because of the machinations of EML and his mother. The
paper now had the mother in their sights as well, recounting
how she went to great lengths to avoid any examination by the
courts in respect of her son's wealth or her part in him evading
the jurisdiction of the English courts.

Another target for Stead was no less a foe than *The Times* of
London. He reported two different ways in which the decisions
of *The Times* had been influenced in the case. The first was when
in 1883 their new-born daughter was very ill Mildred tried to
contact EML by an appeal in *The Times*'s classified advertisements

as both EML's mother and his solicitors were ignoring her pleas. Nothing appeared. She waited a week and then had to write to them, only to discover that EML's solicitors had intervened. A breach of confidentiality must have occurred to enable them to do so. *The Times* would not publish the item in the format she had submitted it, nor had it advised her of their decision. The second relates to the reporting of the court proceedings over the years, which, remarkably, barely appeared in *The Times* at all.

The reason the *Gazette* was running the story at all, according to Stead, is that in February 1887, Mildred finally got her mother-in-law into court. The aim was to establish that the goods at Southampton belonged to EML. Even here Mildred was thwarted as the court found in favour of the mother on the basis of her own sworn testimony that the goods, including the animals, were hers.

> [Desperate] she [Mildred] walked, heedless of all else, from the Law courts up the Strand; when, hardly knowing how it happened, she found herself in Northumberland Street opposite the office of the *Pall Mall Gazette*. She looked wistfully up at the windows. Six months before she had written praying for help, and she had received a promise to insert a statement of her case if she sent it. She had not sent it, but had proposed a personal interview, to which no answer had been returned. The old idea came back: 'If he would take up my case perhaps something might be done'. And with the vaguest idea of what could be done or how her case could be taken up, she entered the office and asked for the editor, very much as a drowning man clutches at a straw.

Stead is not a man for modesty when it comes to telling his readers how the 'editors of the twelve daily papers of London' can help address the wrongs suffered by citizens:

> Mrs Langworthy lacked everything. So she came with the

A typical court scene c.1900. Courtesy of www.edwardianpromenade.com

rest, climbed the familiar stairs up which come statesmen and diplomatists, soldiers and agitators and all the motley crew to whom publicity is as the breath of life. Men with a grievance and women in despair flock to the offices of the twelve as pilgrims to a shrine. For the editor is like Sandalphon in the Rabbinical legend – Sandalphon the angel of prayer. It is a prosaic rendering no doubt. For he has much to do besides listening to the sounds that ascend from below –

> From the hearts that are broken with losses
> And weary with dragging the crosses
> Too heavy for Mortals to bear

And sometimes, although all too seldom, out of the moaning cry that all day long assails his ears, he is able to convey an articulate petition to the ears of Demos himself.

To give Stead his due, though, his research and analysis of the case was meticulous even if wrapped up in what we would now regard as very overblown language. On Wednesday 11 May 1887 the *Gazette* led with the headline, 'How to Help Mrs Langworthy'

THE
PALL MALL GAZETTE
An Evening Newspaper and Review.

No. 6910.—Vol. XLV. **WEDNESDAY, MAY 11, 1887.** Price One Penny.

HOW TO HELP MRS. LANGWORTHY.

Our "Strange True Story" is ended to-day, and the public is at last in possession of the facts of the Langworthy marriage. We have never printed any narrative concerning any individual which has excited so deep an interest and commanded so sustained an attention. It is simply a small segment hewn out of the palpitating, quivering body politic, and exhibited to the view of all men under the microscope of the press. It is a bit of the realism of reality, instinct with the deep human interest that pertains to every struggle which the individual makes against an apparently inexorable destiny. Whatever else it may have failed to do, it has at least served the purpose of all true tragedy, and purified the soul by rousing into keener vitality the emotions of pity and of awe.

But it is not merely pity and tender compassion which the Langworthy marriage excites, but fierce indignation and burning shame. Andromeda chained helplessly to the rock to be devoured at the leisure of some hideous monster of the deep is a favourite subject for artists and painters who seek in the ancient mythologies in the past the inspiration that is not lacking in realities of the present. But here we have no fabled victim of an imaginary doom, nor is the devouring monster an idle myth. In these last four years this narrative has shown us how an Irish lady, fair to look upon, nicely nurtured in a gentle home, cultured beyond most of her sex, has been slowly, ruthlessly hunted from pillar to post, from one court to another, ever making a gallant and heroic fight, but driven ever nearer and nearer to the spot where, chained by want and paralyzed by despair, she would, as an unresisting victim, wait her doom. It is a pitiful and tragic spectacle, a woman trying in vain to escape, but ever hunted back, not by the furies, but by the sleuthhounds of debt, destitution, and of despair. In vain at each turning-point in this strange and hideous chase our Judges expressed the indignation which the spectacle inspires in every human heart. They were powerless to intervene. All that they could do was to lay down the laws of the game, and to decree penalties for their violation—penalties which they could not enforce. And all around the ring in which the tortured woman was being done to death stood the respectable solicitors and the most eminent Q.C.'s, who employed their forensic skill and professional reputation in thrusting her back to her pursuers, at the bidding of the man who, far away in the Argentine, waited the arrival of the glad tidings that his agents had executed his instructions, and that his wife would trouble him no more. It is a ghastly picture of the foulest realities of life.

What a mockery upon Law and Justice, to say nothing of the sacred principles of Chivalry and Christianity, is the fact that this has actually taken place in the very centre of London without eliciting more than a passing protest from an indignant judge! The press was silent, the public apathetic. Nay, were it possible to conceive such a thing, were Mr. Langworthy even more utterly lost to all human feeling, he would still find no difficulty in finding the ablest barristers to strain the resources of their rhetoric and exhaust their innuendo in crushing the miserable victim of a millionaire's selfishness. That may be in the nature of things, and, according to the ethics of an honourable profession, it may be all right. But the Langworthy marriage has raised another question, and a very serious one for the lawyers. When an honest and respectable solicitor finds that he has been instructed falsely by a disreputable client, what is the course which that solicitor ought to pursue? When these false instructions only concern the affairs of the client, the solicitor may decide, according to his inclination or caprice, whether or not he will condone the want of confidence shown by his client, or whether he will resent it by refusing to act any further for a man who lies even to his confidential advisers. But when the false instructions given to a solicitor lead that solicitor to swear an affidavit that defeats the ends of justice and inflicts cruel injury upon an innocent person, then has that solicitor any alternative but to refuse to hold any further relations with a client who has so disgracefully deceived him? Such at least is one of the questions which are raised by this case—a question on which the lawyers will find the great public has a very decided opinion, an opinion which if it had been shared by Messrs. Bircham would have rendered it impossible for them to act for

their client after Mr. Langworthy's lie in the affidavit that defeated Mrs. Langworthy's first application for alimony.

But we are less concerned to-day about the ethics of solicitors than with the practical duty of giving tangible assistance to the lady whose wrongs we rejoice to have been the means of setting forth before the public. Evil and infamous as has been the treatment to which she has been subjected in the past, the shame and the disgrace attaching to it are confined to the narrow circle of those who were more or less accessory to the injustice. But now that the public at large is familiar with the treatment to which she has been subjected the responsibility for a continuance of her sufferings can no longer be regarded as solely the affair of Mr. Langworthy. Thousands and tens of thousands have followed with intense interest and sympathy the story of Mrs. Langworthy's indomitable struggle, and have burned with fierce indignation against her brutal husband. Sympathy and indignation, however, are mere froth unless they lead to action, and fortunately there is no difficulty in giving practical effect to both emotions by the same means. Mr. Langworthy is defiant because he is rich and Mrs. Langworthy is poor. She has not even the wherewithal with which to prosecute her suit. She has not even the wherewithal to keep body and soul together. That, however, can easily be remedied, and must be remedied forthwith. We appeal, therefore, to all those who in any way are interested, whether on public or on private grounds, in the cause to subscribe to the Langworthy Defence Fund, which the proprietors of the *Pall Mall Gazette* will head with a subscription of one hundred guineas. The object of this fund will be to defend the legal rights and claims of Mrs. Langworthy and her child, to maintain Mrs. Langworthy until such time as she can secure the payment of her alimony and to aid in compelling Mr. Edward Martin Langworthy to comply with the orders of the Court. All the money subscribed, without any deduction for advertising or other expenses, will be vested in trustees to be hereafter named, who will appropriate it solely to the ends for which it has been subscribed, and not to the defraying of any outstanding costs, claims, or liabilities.

The Trustees and the Committee will be selected from the subscribers, and the disposition of the fund will be in their hands. Meanwhile, all subscriptions sent in to the Treasurer of the Langworthy Fund, *Pall Mall Gazette* Office, Northumberland-street, Strand, will be acknowledged in our columns. The first list of subscriptions will appear to-morrow.

Strange True Stories of To-Day.

THE LANGWORTHY MARRIAGE.

CHAPTER LXXI.—A Friend in Need.

When Mrs. Langworthy's engagement at Messrs. Stuart's stall at the Royal Agricultural Hall, Islington, came to an end, she met with a pleasant surprise. She was grieving over the stoppage of two days' pay from her week's wage, owing to her inevitable absence at the Bankruptcy Court, when a gentleman asked her if she was permanently engaged with Messrs. Stuart. On hearing that she was not, he said that Messrs. Homan and Rodgers, of 17, Gracechurch-street, were wanting some one to take charge of a stall at the Manchester Exhibition, and recommended her to apply for the post. She had often noticed the handsome stand of the firm. The jury had awarded it a gold medal, but she remembered it far more for the occasional kindly courtesies which she had received from the exhibitors than from the beauty and variety of the exhibits.

That night she wrote saying that she urgently needed immediate work. Mr. Ernest Homan replied, sending her £1,000 envelopes to be addressed at 2s. per 100, paying for the same in advance. About this time comfortable lodgings were secured for her in a pleasant suburb, and she was at last free from the pressure of immediate want.

Seldom was more timely aid more delicately given. Mr. Ernest Homan assured her that when she finished addressing the circulars he would guarantee her sufficient work to bring in £1 a week until something more permanent turned up. Mr. Julius Homan, his father, insisted on sending her £10, with which she was able to replenish her wardrobe, and soon afterwards sent her delicacies, of which in her

---

'How to Help Mrs Langworthy', *Pall Mall Gazette*, 11 May 1887.
British Library Newspapers, http://tinyurl.galegroup.com/tinyurl/6iYmE9. Accessed 5 July 2018.

having concluded their reporting of the case the day before. After another attack on EML and the legal profession, Stead announced the establishment of the 'Langworthy Defence Fund' which the proprietors of the *Gazette* were priming with a donation of 100 guineas. Over the succeeding days, a list of subscribers was published, most donating between one and five guineas, but the full range was £25 down to 1 shilling. Questions about the conduct of the legal proceedings in the case were raised in the House of Commons on 12 May. By 18 May the *Gazette* reported that the Fund had topped £1,000 and Stead was goading the barristers who had profited from the case to make a donation. He also began to quote other newspapers' reporting in the case, including the *South American Journal*. As donations rolled in, the *Gazette* continued to publicise all efforts by the family to reach a financial settlement and bring the story to an end. On 24 May, under the leading headline 'The Lady, the Lawyers and the Public' Stead announced the publication of a *Pall Mall Gazette* 'Extra', illustrated, priced at sixpence called 'The Langworthy Marriage'.

Stead must have felt vindicated and triumphant. He had, in the view of his biographer, Robinson, successfully conducted the first modern tabloid campaign.

There are other 'Strange But True' matters associated with this saga.

In 1898 many papers carried reports of EML's suicide. For example, *The Guardian* said that he shot and wounded himself in the Grand Hotel in Paris in November 1898. He had gone there with Mildred and their daughter a few days before. His wife 'died suddenly' the day after he had sent his daughter back to England.

> Some hours afterwards a report of firearms resounded from his room [*The Guardian* reported] and the servants, rushing in, found Mr Langworthy lying wounded on the floor. He had shot himself, his mind having apparently been unhinged by the death of his wife.

He died soon afterwards. Mr Langworthy (the Paris telegram says) was sixty and his wife about ten years his junior. Before killing himself with a fowling-piece he wrote several letters, including one to the Police Comissary. He explained to him that he had no longer any object in his life and was disgusted with it . . . Can it be that Mr and Mrs Langworthy had at last made up their differences and were living together?

Many other reports of this event offer this image of a tragic reconciliation, but EML was nowhere to be seen when Mildred, resident in Claremont Road, Folkestone, appeared before the East Kent Bankruptcy Court in December 1895. It seems that the court took a dim view that in the eight years since she achieved her settlement from EML she had spent 'no less a sum than £9,000 . . . it would appear that the debtor has been very extravagant.'

Robinson, in his biography of Stead, was quite blunt, affirming that EML had murdered Mildred before killing himself.

Late in his saga of Langworthy (26 May), Stead reported that 'An Able Seaman' (Stead's quotation marks) had written offering to give particulars of the last voyage EML had made with his first wife. She was the Lady Alice Louisa Pery, daughter of the

---

16   *PALL MALL GAZETTE*   [May 26, 1887.

STRANGE   TRUE   STORIES   OF   TO-DAY.

Crown 4to.   70 pp.   Price Sixpence.   Post free, Sevenpence-halfpenny.

R E A D Y   T H I S   D A Y,

THE   LANGWORTHY   MARRIAGE.

With a Cabinet Photograph of Mrs. EDWARD M. LANGWORTHY,
AUTOGRAPH, and NUMEROUS PORTRAITS.

"PALL MALL GAZETTE" OFFICE, 2, NORTHUMBERLAND STREET, STRAND, LONDON, W.C.

'Advertisements & Notices', *Pall Mall Gazette*, 26 May 1887.
British Library Newspapers, http://tinyurl.galegroup.com/tinyurl/6iYtt0. Accessed 5 July 2018.

second Earl of Limerick. Her first marriage, in 1868, to Capt.
Percy Hughes Hewitt, a captain in the 6th Dragoon Guards was
annulled on the grounds of non-consummation in 1872. She
married EML in March 1874 and she died on 15 September 1876,
aged thirty, at sea. Stead claimed that EML had once shut her up
in a lunatic asylum 'and shipped her home from India much as
he shipped Mrs Langworthy from Buenos Aires.'

W. T. Stead remained active as a campaigner and journalist,
albeit with his best years behind him, when, on a fateful day in
1912 he drowned on RMS *Titanic*.

On a happier note, the daughter of EML and Mildred,
Elizabeth Gladys Langworthy survived all the trials and
tribulations in her mother's womb and beyond and went on to
marry the Hon. Charles Richard Molesworth, 10th Viscount
Molesworth, and had three children. She lived until 1974. She is
the grandmother of the current viscount.

* * *

The entire Langworthy family will have been appalled at EML
and the whole scandal, bringing the family name into disrepute
after so many years building both a fortune and good reputation
in Manchester. ERL in particular had clearly wanted to leave
a legacy of philanthropy associated with the family name. For
reasons not known to us he bequeathed to EML almost three
times what George and his brothers received (over £11 million
at today's values). As it was ERL who had made money in South
America perhaps EML had been guided by his uncle in making
initial investments there as EML will have inherited from his
father before his uncle's death. Stead was able to portray him as a
scoundrel using his wealth both to abuse and try to deny justice
to a young woman who bore him a child. Stead was fiercely
critical of EML's mother for remaining resolutely on her son's
side and briefly attacked 'The Langworthy Clan', though only

naming ERL's widow, who was the only member of the family
bearing the name Langworthy and still permanently living in
Manchester

By the standards of public morality of the time Mildred's
behaviour would have seemed totally reckless and foolish however
much Stead tried to portray her as an innocent victim. The kind
of reporting we now called 'tabloid' journalism needs villains
and victims and heroes. In this tale perhaps Stead himself is
the hero, Mildred of course the victim, and EML the villain.
Nevertheless, there were other ways that wealthy men covered
up their waywardness and EML seems to have been particularly
cruel and heartless. Perhaps George's younger brother, too,
was complicit. Stead reports him as accompanying EML on
the fateful voyage first to Lisbon and then on to Buenos Aires.
Although Edward settled in British Columbia he came to own
property in Argentina, perhaps acquiring it from EML when the
latter was divesting himself of assets to declare himself bankrupt
to the courts in London.

Given George's behaviour both as a soldier and philanthropist
in Spain it is safe to assume that he would have shuddered at the
thought of his cousin's behaviour towards Mildred however much
the family will have blamed her for the scandal and particularly
for using a newspaper in the way that she did. His family's
treatment of Mildred stands in stark contrast to the experience
of a young British woman who similarly found herself pregnant
and unmarried and whom George was to meet in Spain in 1928.

CHAPTER SIX
India

When Second Lieutenant George Langworthy of the 7th (Princess Royal's) Dragoon Guards set sail for India in 1887 there are one or two things he will have been glad to leave behind. One would be the scandal surrounding his cousin. He supposed it would come up in conversations in the regiment, but hopefully would soon pass, so removed from England would he be. The second thing was the bruises his initial training had brought him. George will have thought himself quite an accomplished horseman by the time he joined the regiment. Nothing could have prepared him for his initiation into regimental horsemanship. Sir Winston Churchill, who joined a cavalry regiment about the same time recalls:

> Mounting and dismounting from a bare-backed horse at the trot or canter; jumping a high bar without stirrups or even a saddle, sometimes with hands clasped behind one's back; jogging at a fast trot with nothing but the horse's hide between your knees . . . Many a time did I pick myself up shaken and sore . . .[1]

---

1   I have chosen, in the main, to use the terminology, such as the names of towns, used by the British at the time, often adding the modern equivalent in brackets. The uprising that the British called the Indian mutiny of 1857 is known in modern India as the First War of Independence. The original British term relates to the fact that the uprising involved Indian members of the Bengal Army.

George was not the only new addition to the regiment. The edition of the *London Gazette* which carried news of George's appointment as a second lieutenant in the regiment on augmentation announced that Lt C.W. Battine from the 3rd Battalion the Royal Welsh Fusiliers had achieved the same position. The 7th (The Princess Royal's) Dragoon Guards were heavy cavalry which is a class of cavalry whose primary role was to engage in direct combat with enemy forces, and are heavily armed and armoured compared to light cavalry. They were generally mounted on large powerful horses. Light cavalry, often called Light Horse were comparatively lightly armed. The role of the light cavalry was primarily reconnaissance, screening, skirmishing, raiding and most importantly, communications.

The journey by steam ship from England to India took about three weeks now that the Suez Canal had been completed, avoiding the long and dangerous voyage around the southern tip of Africa. As they entered the Canal, the world seemed to take on a different character. The sailing boats they glimpsed from the ship were rigged differently. The voices, the cries, seemed different. It was the first sense of the reality of the British Empire. It was only five years since the British had gained control of the canal as well as controlling Egypt and Sudan and it must have seemed like genuine evidence of the belief all children of George's time had been brought up with: Britain's dominance in the world. By now George will have digested the campaigns and triumphs of his regiment, so he will have felt a sense of pride to know that the regiment had a hand in seizing control of the Canal from the French in 1882. Construction of the Canal had been led by the French who had a majority shareholding. The 'khedive' or governor (at the time Egypt was a vassal state of the Ottoman Empire) sold his 44 per cent share in the Canal in 1875 as he could not pay his debts. Unrest in Egypt over the foreign ownership of the Canal led to the invasion of 1882 to protect British interests.

Sketch 7th Dragoon Guards entering the Suez Canal in 1882.
Copyright © Royal Dragoon Guards Collection, York Army Museum

Members of the regiment on horse in front of Sphinx, 1882.
Copyright © Royal Dragoon Guards Collection, York Army Museum.

The change in the climate will have become more obvious too. Sleeping on deck was the only way to avoid the stifling heat of the cabins as the ship sailed towards its destination. Once George's ship arrived in Bombay (now Mumbai) the water of the huge landlocked harbour would have been alive with rowing boats, sailcraft and tugs ready to guide the ship to its mooring, the sights and sounds and smells bewildering. On the quayside a press of humanity would push and heave about, shouting in different languages and dialects, although George would not have been able to pick one out from another. A dazzling array of colours, from the women's saris to the produce and spices for sale on every conceivable surface, would greet his eyes. First stop was a rest camp, such as the one at Poona (now Pune) about one hundred miles inland from Bombay. After a first night's rest, George will have been greeted by Indians seeking to be his butler, dressing-boy and head *syce* (groom). Subalterns like George would be expected to employ three such servants and applicants would all be able to offer testimonials from officers who had since left for England:

> If you liked to be waited on and relieved of home worries India . . . was perfection. All you had to do was hand over all your uniform and clothes to the dressing boy, your ponies to the *syce* and your money to the butler and you need never trouble any more . . . No toil was too hard, no hours were too long, no dangers too great for their unruffled calm or their unfailing care. Princes could live no better than we.

So wrote Winston Churchill of the life of the lowliest British officer in the Raj. Now equipped with his own entourage George faced a train journey of 350 miles (modest by Indian standards) to the regiment's base at Mhow. At the stations *en route* the same thronging crowds and noise would have greeted him, offering all kinds of things for sale. The first class carriages in which

Europeans travelled were very comfortable as the railway gauge was wide. The lack of corridors meant that they could seem more like sitting rooms on wheels. At stops, one of his servants would appear from third class to minister to any needs he might have. George could sit back and look out undisturbed at the featureless plains, then buffaloes, villages, temples and mosques as the train headed northwards and inland until he arrived at Mhow, his new home. He would now need to organise himself some living accommodation.

'No quarters are provided for the officers. They draw instead a lodging allowance . . . All around the cavalry mess lies a suburb of roomy one-storeyed bungalows standing in their own walled grounds and gardens.' So describes Churchill the arrangements at Bangalore where he was posted, but George would have encountered similar accommodation at Mhow. Churchill goes on: 'We three [he quartered with two other new subalterns as George might have done with Battine] pooling all our resources took a palatial bungalow, all pink and white with heavy tiled roof and deep verandahs sustained by white plaster columns.'

George would have got to know the interior of his bungalow very well in his first months at Mhow. In the early morning the horses would be exercised, there would be drills and individual training. By ten o'clock or half-past it was considered too hot to do anything other than retreat to the bungalow only emerging for lunch. That first year George would have wondered if the stifling heat would ever abate. Reed matting (*khas-khas tattis*) was hung over the doorways and soaked in water to try and keep the temperature down and supplement the efforts of the *punkah-wallahs* to keep the air moving with their creaking fans. Well into the 1930s it was considered dangerous for the British to be out in the sun during the midday hours. After about five o'clock the place would come alive and the horses would be exercised again. After a hot bath and perhaps some more rest, drinks and dinner would be at about 8.30 p.m. To detract from this easy lifestyle,

Bungalow Umballa. Courtesy of the British Library.

apart from the oppressive heat, there was the ever-present danger of disease: cholera, typhoid, malaria and dysentery were an accepted part of life as medical science still had little to combat these diseases, and every year hundreds if not thousands of the British, military and civilian alike met an untimely death.

George may have had to wait a while to meet some of his fellow officers. Most took leave in the summer months if they could, to escape the heat on the plains, which was intolerable until the monsoons broke. They may have gone home to England or travelled up to the hills in the north. His first winter will have brought relief and, by comparison, excitement. On 14 December 1887 the regiment set off on a route march. The first leg was about 260 miles to Rupaheli which took four weeks. Here they stayed for almost three weeks on a camp of exercise before setting off again to Umballa (now Ambala), a distance of five hundred miles which took them through Jeypore (now Jaipur), Muttra (now Mathura) and Delhi. Umballa lies between Delhi and Simla (now alternatively spelt Shimla). They arrived in Umballa on 23 March and that became George's base for three and a half years. In his book *Sahib*, Richard Holmes reproduces a description of Umballa written by a Major Bayley in 1854. This was three years before what the British called the Indian Mutiny, but Churchill's later description of typical accommodation does not indicate a lot of change. Originally in India, troops were quartered in forts, but as the East India Company (which controlled large parts of India until the British Crown took over after the 1857 uprising) extended its power, military cantonments of purpose-built barracks were formed outside towns usually alongside the civil lines that housed the official Europeans. By the 1880s when George arrived, the Umballa cantonment covered forty-eight square miles, built on a grid pattern. It included a church, St Pauls, and a cemetery. Bayley's description gives a flavour of the arrangements:

> On the extreme left space was allotted for three regiments of native infantry, and on their right for a regiment of European infantry, on whose right European cavalry were placed; in whose right rear were the native cavalry; in some distance in rear of the infantry line was the civil station.
>
> All along the front, which at Umballa was about a mile and a half long, barracks for the Europeans and mud huts called 'lines' for Indians were constructed; the officers being considerably allowed the option of living in their tents or building bungalows for themselves. Under these circumstances they would receive increased allowances of pay which went towards the rent of a house when one was built. Sooner or later, houses sprang up on the ground allotted to the different corps. Most of these were built by the officers themselves, though a few were the property of European or native speculators – and a very good investment they were, as they were seldom unoccupied, and a house which had cost £200 to build let easily for £60 a year. Officers who had been obliged to build were only too glad to recover some of their

money, when they got the route for a distant station, and so most of the bungalows eventually became the property of shopkeepers and merchants resident there.

The following winter, 1888, George's regiment undertook a twelve-day march to Delhi to take part in a camp of exercise and another in the winter of 1891 at Allygarh (now Aligarh) with divisional manoeuvres to Meerut and on to Muttra.

Obviously the purpose of these military activities was to keep the regiment active in the event of them being called to action. These apart, much of life will have been structured around sport and games, competitive activities to maintain and develop military skills. As George was in a cavalry regiment, many of the activities reflected the skills needed by a mounted soldier. There were, for example, competitions in tent-pegging and lime cutting. The first of these involved charging at full gallop holding a lance with which to lift a tent peg from the ground. The idea was that

Cantonment Umballa. Courtesy of the British Library.

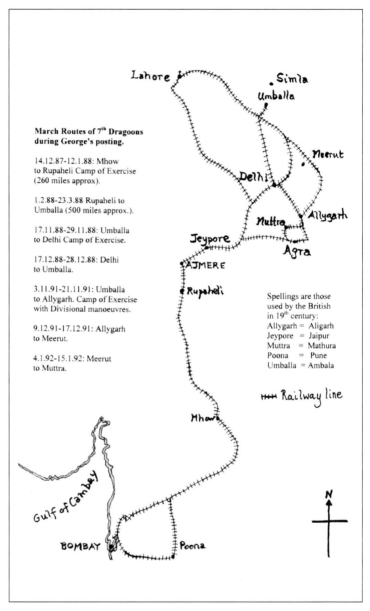

Map of part of India showing principal towns and railways relevant to George's posting. Copyright © Gill Shapton.

Camp at Aligarh. Copyright © Royal Dragoon Guards Collection, York Army Museum

pulling the pegs from an enemy's tent in a surprise raid would cause the enemy's tent to collapse resulting in confusion. It's not known if this tactic was ever used in combat, but it certainly took some skill and accuracy. Lime-cutting or -splitting was a skill with sword: a lime (or lemon) was set upon a pole staked in the ground and the mounted competitor charged at it, aiming to split the lime with his sword. Competition results in the regimental gazette show that George was good at these events often achieving first or second place. He was equally good at more recognisable sports such as sword-fencing and horse-racing. Most of the sports were practised by officers and men alike but separately. Intra-regimental competition was supplemented by inter-regimental competition. Some regard polo as the toughest of the sports and one which, naturally, is mainly the preserve of cavalry regiments. In fact, just before the regiment set off on its winter 1887 march from Mhow they learned that a lieutenant in another regiment had been killed playing polo. The competitions between regiments would often attract spectators, and arguably the spectators the competitors were most eager to impress were not commanding officers but young women.

Many young women came out to India expressly in search

of a husband. The practice had started under the East India Company. When the Crown took over running India in 1858 the number of young women making the journey steadily increased and then after the journey time was cut by the opening of the Suez Canal in 1869, numbers took off. Most made the journey at the beginning of the cold weather, that is to say they would leave England in the autumn. In the days of the East India Company the ships carrying women out were given the nickname 'The Fishing Fleet' and this name stuck after the beginning of the Raj. This practice is well researched and documented by Anne de Courcy in her book of that name. She offers an insight into the social life of the British in India at that time

The practice of 'husband-hunting' in India was a response to the harsh facts of nineteenth century life at home. The proportion of unmarried women in Victorian Britain was surprisingly high: between 1851 and 1911 about one third of women aged twenty-five to thirty-five were unmarried. By the age of twenty-five a woman could come to be regarded as 'on the shelf'. For middle-class women, spinsterhood meant earning a pittance as a companion, governess or teacher or living off the charity of a male relative. A good marriage was the ideal and India was full of young men with prospects. Military and civilian careers alike could bring great rewards.

Charles Arthur Roe, the father of the woman who would become George's wife, was a member of the elite Indian Civil Service. There were only about one thousand of them and they were the cream of Oxbridge graduates selected to become government officials, administrators, judges, collectors and commissioners. When Charles set sail for India in 1862 he knew that there was no home leave for the first eight years. The rule in the Indian Civil Service was that no one married before the age of thirty. To do so usually meant the loss of their post or if permission was reluctantly granted they would suffer some form of financial penalty. Charles was appointed to the post of assistant commissioner of the Punjab. He must have been very highly regarded to be given permission to marry in July 1865 when he had not even reached his twenty-fourth birthday. The exact date of birth of his wife, Elizabeth Gaskell, is not known but the year is given as 1848, making her seventeen when she married. She was born in Kidderpore. The first of her six surviving children was born the following year. Charles, a law graduate, finished his career as chief justice of the Lahore High Court and was knighted in 1897, the year before he retired.

A proportion of the girls going out to India were returning to their families after a childhood in England. It is not known if this was the experience of Elizabeth Gaskell, but it was true of George's future wife, Annie Roe, and her older sister, Frances. The reason was set out clearly by Sir Joseph Fayrer of the Bengal Medical Service:

> It has long been known to the English in India that children may be kept in that country up to five, six or seven years of age without any deterioration, physical or moral . . . But [to do so] after that age . . . is always a doubtful proceeding. The child must be sent to England or it will deteriorate physically and morally.

In the 1881 census Annie (aged nine) and Frances (aged fourteen) are in the village of Tarrant Rushton in Dorset in the household of the Reverend James Penny and his wife, their 'Aunt Moggie', the sister of their father who was born in the nearby town of Blandford Forum. The girls were probably lucky to be there; some Raj children were lodged in boarding houses that catered specifically for the offspring of officials in the Raj, or with unloving relatives or simply placed in boarding schools where they had to remain in school holidays while everyone else went home.

By the time George reached India, Frances, the only sister of his future wife, had been married for two years. She had married

Annie with her older sister, Frances, in   A young Annie.
India. Courtesy of Remi Fernandez Campoy.   Courtesy of Remi Fernandez Campoy.

James McCrone Douie in the pro-cathedral in Lahore in April 1885.
Frances was eleven weeks short of her nineteenth birthday when
she married. This was not unusual – her mother had married at
seventeen. Frances' parents will have known Douie and regarded
him as a suitable husband. It is even possible that Frances' brother
Reginald knew Douie from university. They were both at Balliol
College, Oxford, and both left England in the same year, 1876, but
Reginald's destination was Australia. Like his future father-in-law,
Douie joined the Indian Civil Service and came to the Punjab where
Charles Roe was Assistant Commissioner. Douie would spend his
whole career there becoming Chief Secretary to the government of
the Punjab and was knighted in the year of his retirement, 1911. He
was twelve years older than Frances. Engagements were often quite
short in India at that time. They would go on to have six surviving
children, though it is possible that Frances gave birth to ten, perhaps
four dying at birth or in early infancy. The reason for suggesting this

Charles and Elizabeth Roe with family and friends in Lahore, Feb 1891. From
left to right: Annie's cousin from Dorset; the wife of the photographer; Frances'
husband; Mrs and Mr Roe; Frances; the family doctor; Annie. Mrs Roe would
die four months later. (The image is from the collection of Walter Hume, Chief
Commissioner of Lands for Queensland Australia. It is very likely that he knew
Reginald Roe – Charles' brother – as colonial European Queensland was a small
circle, especially for the families of wealth and power. Reginald was headmaster
of Brisbane Grammar School at the time the photograph was taken, but in 1911 he
became Vice Chancellor of the University of Queensland.)
Courtesy of University of Queensland, Hume Collection, Firth Library

is that her last child was given the name Decima, with Langworthy
as her middle name, perhaps in celebration of her little sister Annie
marrying in 1899, or in tribute to George, for reasons which will
become apparent later.

In her book *The Fishing Fleet* Anne de Courcy gives a clear
account of the inter-relationship between military expertise, sport
and socialising with a view to marriage. 'Army officers were also a
catch'; again the under thirty rule applied. This meant that most
had to be captains before they could start to look for a wife. The
informal rule in the army was: 'subalterns cannot marry, captains
may marry, majors should marry, colonels must marry.' As George

was under thirty and a subaltern when he was in India (he became a captain in 1896 when he was back in England), marriage was not on the cards. This was despite him being in the highest social strata of the army: 'the good regiments, in particular the cavalry who were, on the whole richer than most of their contemporaries – often young men who had joined because they were attracted by the hunting and polo that were then considered a part of cavalry life.'

Most officers would have attended British public schools where sport was entrenched into the school week – and weekend as most would have been boarders. In India hunting featured strongly alongside the field sports. Packs of foxhounds were brought out from England and traditional English riding outfits would be worn even if the prey was jackal. An invitation to a tiger shoot on elephants with a maharajah would be much valued. For army officers sport 'was regarded as mental and physical preparation for war-cavalry commanders believed that the best way to learn the skills of the cavalry charge was in the hunting field, while pig-sticking taught accuracy with a lance.'

Polo originated in India. 'In some stations there were chukkas every day, with matches, tournaments and intense rivalry – being one of the four-man regimental polo team was every young officer's dream.' One writer declared that:

> The hardest and most dangerous time was playing polo on the dry hard ground where bones got broken, heads bashed and that winter 'one death'; all bumps and accidents, even fatalities accepted as part of the game . . . Play starts off with a spurt of dust and rattle of hoofs on the iron ground, and in no time at all all that could be seen was the arc of a swinging stick through billows of white dust. As the tournament progressed the games got tougher, the finals becoming a deadly battle.

Vigorous sport was also meant to distract the young male from sex since marriage was out of the question but social events were almost non-stop during the winter:

When the cold weather began in mid-October it was the signal for four months of non-stop gaiety – race weeks, polo weeks, ICS weeks, rugger weeks, cricket weeks, rowing weeks, horse shows, gymkhanas, paperchases, moonlight picnics, garden parties and constant dinner and cocktail parties.

A paperchase was a paper trail which riders on horseback would follow over jumps of mud walls and coconut leaves like a point to point in England. There was plenty of dancing, riding, swimming, picnics, amateur theatricals, choir-singing, snipe-shooting . . . the list was endless.

The most beautiful girls were known as Week Queens: girls asked to all the 'Weeks' of the cold-weather season – Calcutta Week, Lahore Week, Meerut Week, Rawalpindi Week, Delhi Week, each with horse shows, polo, gymkhanas, tent-pegging contests, tennis tournaments, dances, dinners, fancy dress balls, cocktail parties every night . . . There was always a New Years' day parade with cavalry and infantry marching and galloping across dusty parade grounds.

Racecourse at Secunderabad. Copyright © Royal Dragoon Guards Collection, York Army Museum

In summer, by contrast, the British took to the hills. The small towns and stations afforded wives, children and anyone on leave a respite from the heat of the plains. The best known station was Simla which from 1864 became the summer capital of British India as it was the hill station for Calcutta (which was the capital before New Delhi). The buildings in Simla ranged from Tudorbethan to neo-Gothic via Swiss chalet. To this day, the main street has a distinctly Scottish air. Flowers familiar from Britain could be grown: sweet peas, petunias, wisteria, wallflowers, phlox, lilac . . . Love affairs and flirtations flourished as well, with husbands often absent and plenty of unmarried young officers and officials. As Kipling put it 'every Jack has someone else's Jill'.

George probably had a wonderful time in India. A bit of soldiering, plenty of hunting, tennis perhaps (he had a court made on his property in Spain), a few flirtations. Thanks to the rail network, army officers were highly mobile, moving around the country for sporting or social events. He was in the right part of the country to spend time in Lahore, where the Roes lived, but as we have learned, he was the wrong age and rank to marry. He may or may not have met Annie in India. If he did, the issue of marriage may have been under consideration for a future date; Annie was in her late teens and George was twenty-five in 1890 (still way off the 'thirty-to-marry' rule), but if they did meet, an accident in 1892 mentioned below may have disrupted any romance. In the meantime, George may well have attended at least one wedding: his sister Ida, one year older than him, married in Calcutta on Boxing Day 1890. Her husband, Henry Willock Boileau, was only three years her senior, but Ida was quite an old bride at twenty-six! Henry became the District Superintendent of Bengal in the year he was married. He was to retire from service in India in 1900 (aged thirty-nine) and devote most of his remaining years to fox hunting in Berkshire until his death in 1940.

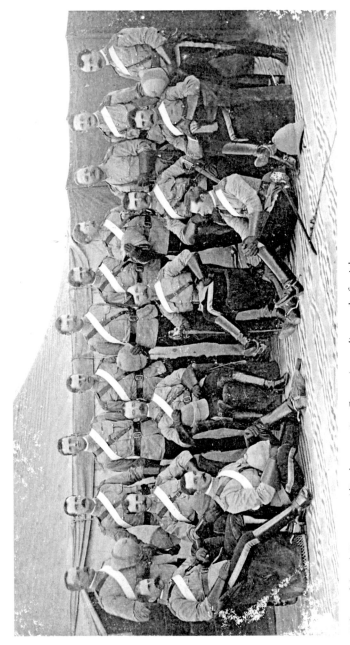

Officers of the 7th Dragoon at Aligarh camp, 1891. George is standing on the far right.
Copyright © Royal Dragoon Guards Collection, York Army Museum.

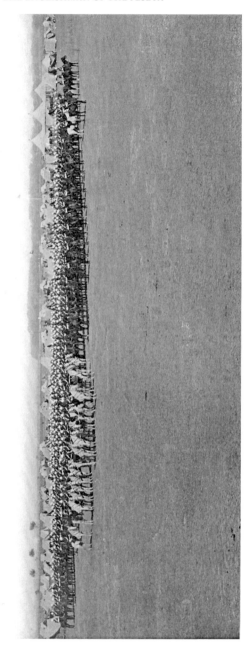

The 7th Dragoons on parade at Aligarh. Copyright © Royal Dragoon Guards Collection, York Army Museum.

George undertook his final camp of exercise with the regiment in November 1891. They marched from Umballa to Aligurh over a period of eighteen days and after divisional manoeuvres from Aligurh to Muttra in December, they completed a second march from Muttra to Mhow in January 1892.

The photograph of officers of the 7th Dragoon Guards in India is interesting as it shows that they were wearing quite plain khaki tunics. But they continued to wear the blue breeches with a gold stripe. The white undress pouch-belt is worn over the brown leather Sam Browne belt, perhaps inspired by the Corps of Guides who dressed in a similar way. The tunics have steel shoulder chains. Their helmets are also khaki and the gauntlets are brown leather, although the boots are black.

George's time in India came to an abrupt halt in October 1892 when he incurred a steeplechase injury and returned to England. By the time he returned to the regiment they were in Egypt. The May 1893 edition of the regimental *Black Horse Gazette* reported that he was still far from well. He managed to attend a regimental dinner in London in June of 1893 as well as attending the races at Ascot as was the custom of cavalry officers. In November the *Gazette* reported he was still on sick leave though he had managed to take a cruise off the coast of Norway.

George next appears in the *Gazette* in January 1894 in the cricket results for his squadron ('B') against 'C' squadron in Egypt where he was bowled for a duck in the first innings but managed two before being dismissed leg before wicket in the second, though he was his squadron's third best bowler (out of four). You may recall he did not feature in his school record as a cricketer. To his credit he features significantly in the *Gazette* in some of the cavalry sports such as lime-cutting, and also as a swordsman.

In other ways, his time with the regiment in Egypt was uneventful. In July 1894 George went on leave and the regiment returned to England in October of that year.

George the swordsman. Courtesy of Remi Fernandez Campoy

CHAPTER SEVEN
England and Marriage

When did George meet Annie? My belief is that they met in England in 1897 though meeting in Lahore or even Simla is a possibility: Umballa, where George spent most of his time in India, had good connections to both places. There is no record of Annie's whereabouts between her nine-year-old self in Dorset in the 1881 census and appearing in a family photograph in Lahore, with her parents and sister in 1891, shortly

A studio portrait of Annie.
Courtesy of Remi Fernandez Campoy

before her mother's death. It may be that, with her only sister already married, she was expected to remain at her father's side after the death of her mother.

Annie would also be able to stay close to her sister as they were both in the Punjab There are records of Frances having five surviving children in the years that Annie seemed to remain in India, and the presence of her only sister would have been a comfort and support. Annie might have met George before he left India in 1892, but we have no record, nor indeed any record of how and when they met at all. There is a record of Annie leaving India for England with her father on the P&O's ship

Britannia at the beginning of May 1897. Annie's father had been awarded a knighthood in March 1897 by letters patent. The news was relayed in the *London Gazette* of 31 March 1897:

> The Queen has been pleased to direct Letters Patent to be passed under the Great Seal of the United Kingdom of Great Britain and Ireland, granting the dignity of a Knight of the said United Kingdom unto the Honourable Charles Arthur Roe, Chief Judge of the Chief Court of the Punjaub [sic].

On 31 May the newly knighted Sir Charles attended a 'levee' (an afternoon, all-male, assembly) hosted by the Prince of Wales. On 21 June George was part of the squadron of his regiment who, with similar detachments from all the other home-based cavalry, were in the Royal Procession from Buckingham Palace to St Paul's Cathedral to celebrate Queen Victoria's Diamond Jubilee. That parade was the first time in their history that the 7th (Princess Royal's) Dragoon Guards, to give the regiment its full title, had caught a glimpse of their titular chief, Princess Victoria (the eldest child of Queen Victoria and Prince Albert. By a curious irony, she married Frederick the Emperor of Germany and bore Kaiser Wilhelm who precipitated the First World War.

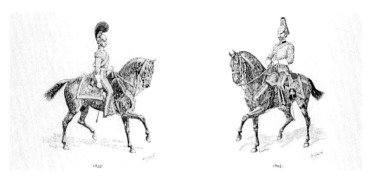

7th Dragoons regimental dress uniform, 1837 and 1897.
Courtesy of Royal Dragoon Guards Collection, York Army Museum

George's yacht *Sayonara*, 1895.
Copyright © Royal Dragoon Guards
Collection, York Army Museum

Regimental staghounds, 1896 (George
second from right). Copyright © Royal Dragoon
Guards Collection, York Army Museum

In February 1898, Annie is on the passenger list of the SS
City of Sparta leaving Liverpool for Calcutta. Perhaps she
had sailed out to help her father prepare for his retirement in
England. On 29 April of that year the *Times of India* reported on
a farewell party to mark Sir Charles' retirement and on 9 May
the paper reported on his departure for England on the P&O
steamer *Egypt*. If Annie did not accompany him on that ship, she
probably followed on soon after and took up residence with him
in Oxford.

Meanwhile, George's career, and sporting pursuits continued
to develop. He owned a yacht which had originally been
purchased by a regimental syndicate, but then bought outright
by him. It was so successful in races one year that changes to
class requirements were made for the following racing season.

After short spells in barracks in Kent and Aldershot, the
regiment moved to a more permanent posting in Norwich. He
did well in riding competitions on his own horse *Surprise*. He
became one of the whips of the regimental staghounds.

The *London Gazette* of 27 October 1896 announced his
promotion to captain.

In October 1898 George was seconded to army staff as aide
de camp to Col. H. F. Grant, CB, Inspector General of Cavalry
in G.B. & Ireland. This was a prestigious appointment. Given

Officers on Salisbury Plain, 1897. (George stands second from right. H. A. Lempiere, witness at the wedding, sits with a cane across his knee.)
Copyright © Royal Dragoon Guards Collection, York Army Museum

Park Lodge, to the right. From J. Greenacombe's Survey of London, vol. 45. Copyright © Historic England

Knightsbridge Barracks, Hyde Park side. From J. Greenacombe's Survey of London, vol. 45. Copyright © Historic England

Annie in her wedding dress. Courtesy of Remi Fernandez Campoy.

that Col. Grant also served with the 7th Dragoon Guards it is possible that the reason for George's appointment is that Grant knew him and was favourably impressed by him. At the time, appointments could be made on this basis. George would have been fairly mobile in his new role, travelling to various Cavalry units in order to inspect them, but his marriage certificate gives his address as Park Lodge, a new development on a site in Knightsbridge, convenient for the Kensington Palace Barracks and for riding in Hyde Park.

Inside, each floor was identically planned as an individual suite; the basement comprised the steward's or housekeeper's rooms, service kitchen and cellarage. The apartments were well appointed with 'every contrivance known to modern club life', including telephones, speaking-tubes, electric bells, electric light (backed up by gas) and a hydraulic passenger lift. The perfect pad for the well-to-do modern bachelor wanting access to Hyde Park.

If he had not already done so, this would have been a propitious time to ask the newly knighted Sir Charles Roe for his daughter's hand in marriage.

On 27 September 1899, Capt. George Langworthy, (aged thirty-four), 7th Dragoon Guards, married Annie Margaret Roe (aged twenty-six) at the Parish Church of the parish of Holy Trinity, in Knightsbridge, London.

The service was conducted by Annie's uncle from Dorset, the Revd James Penny, by then aged seventy-nine. The signature of one of the witnesses, quite possibly George's best man, is recognisable as that of a fellow captain in the 7th, H. A. Lempriere, who would accompany George to South Africa and go on to command the regiment as lieutenant colonel when it was posted from India to fight in the First World War.

Holy Trinity, Knightsbridge, exterior (*left*) and interior (*right*). The church was demolished in 1904.
From J. Greenacombe's *Survey of London*, vol. 45.

Certificate of marriage. From website Find My Past, see https://www.findmypast.co.uk/

CHAPTER EIGHT
South Africa

As George walked his new bride down the aisle of Holy Trinity he would be forgiven for thinking life could not get much better. He had a beautiful wife, the daughter of a knight of the realm. He had a high status role in the élite cavalry of the imperial army of the greatest power on earth. He would be pondering where to buy a house for Annie as his bachelor pad would not be right for her though his absences on duty would mean she would want to be near company. Perhaps a place outside Oxford near to her father; or just a few miles away from Oxford in the Berkshire countryside near cousin Florence; or near her childhood home in Dorset, also not too far from George's brother John; or the new suburbs of London where George's brother Christopher lived.

The only cloud on the horizon at that time was not one seriously to bother George: there was trouble brewing in South Africa. Local conflicts were an inevitable price of empire, but were usually contained: India, 1857; Egypt, 1882, for example. There had been struggles between the European colonising powers in southern Africa throughout the nineteenth century and in 1877 the British had annexed the Transvaal Republic (which was colonised by Boers of Dutch origin) and in 1880 the Boers rose up against the British. A peace treaty was signed in 1881 and the Boers self-governed under British suzerainty (a diluted form of sovereignty). Tensions had increased again and on 11 October 1899, just two weeks after George and Annie's wedding, an ultimatum issued by the Boers to the British expired without the British acceding to the Boers' demands. The British government believed that the conflict would soon be resolved in their favour. In fact, instead of the war being over by Christmas 1899 as was expected in Britain, it proved to be the longest, costliest and bloodiest war fought between 1815 and 1914. It is estimated that the loss of life from the fighting was: Boer 25,000; British, 22,000; African 12,000. The British 'expended' over 400,000 horses, mules and donkeys. Faced with an implacable enemy, the British resorted to tactics which would have shamed British officers and troops educated to consider war an honourable activity. These including the burning of farms and dwellings and the forcing of Boer women and children into concentration camps where many died. The insanitary conditions cost many their lives as hunger and disease ran rampant. Between June 1901 and May 1902, of the 115,000 people in the camps for whites, almost 28,000 died, about 22,000 of them children. The death toll represented about 10 per cent of the Boer population. It is estimated that about 20,000 black Africans died in other, segregated, camps.

Below is the Brigade Order for burning farms published by General Hamilton, 12 December 1900:

Farms should only be burned under the following circumstances:-

(1) When used as a centre of operations by the Boers.

(2) When Boers have sniped our troops from them.

(3) For tactical reasons.

(4) When the farm belongs to a prominent man among the Boers.

(5) When the owner has broken the oath of neutrality without being compelled to.

Horses being embarked at Southampton. Courtesy of Remi Fernandez Campoy

George 'captain for the day'. Courtesy of Remi Fernandez Campoy

SS *Armenian* leaving Southampton 8 February 1900. Courtesy of Royal Dragoon Guards
Collection, York Army Museum

Entraining horses. Courtesy of Remi Fernandez Campoy

There were complex causes to the war but the most immediate was gold. Substantial deposits had been found at Witwatersrand, thirty miles south of Pretoria and there had been an influx of foreigners, mainly British, seeking to mine the gold. All efforts at diplomacy failed, and the Boers, fearing being outnumbered in the lands they regarded as their own (the Transvaal and the Orange Free State), issued their ultimatum for the British to withdraw their forces from the neighbourhood of the borders of the Transvaal. Initially the British sent an expeditionary force of 40,000 to support existing garrisons but the Boers gained the upper hand. Then troop numbers were greatly increased and included George's regiment. The young couple's plans would have to go on hold. Annie went to live with her father in Oxford.

On 8 February 1900 George, as captain of 'B' Squadron of his regiment, left for South Africa with 21 other officers, 507 NCOs and men, 60 chargers, and 403 troop horses on board the SS *Armenian*.

They travelled to Southampton from the barracks at Aldershot on a night so cold that several men contracted pneumonia and one soldier was to die of pleurisy *en route* to South Africa as a consequence of that night. Three more died of pneumonia before the voyage was over.

The *Armenian* was a cattle boat that usually sailed between Liverpool and Boston and one of George's fellow officers laughingly recorded that the horses had better accommodation than the men.

They finally arrived at Cape Town at the beginning of March. From there they travelled by train to de Aar.

Armed with swords and carbines and dressed in khaki uniforms, they formed the 4th Cavalry Brigade together with the 8th and 14th Hussars under the command of Major-General Dickson. They were employed in patrolling and reconnoitring near Bloemfontein. It was on one such patrol that the regiment suffered its first death, one of George's men. A patrol under one of George's lieutenants, Caillard, set out on 7 April and was fired

Private Best.
Courtesy of Remi Fernandez Campoy

on at close range from a farmhouse. One man was wounded and Private Best was shot dead, a shilling which he had in his belt being driven right through his body. A photograph of Private Best, taken in a studio in London, remained in George's possession throughout his life, the date and place of Private Best's death written in pencil on the back.

By the end of April the regiment were bearded and dirty. They fought as mounted infantry because Boer tactics did not allow for set piece cavalry actions. 'A' and 'B' Squadrons fought a dismounted skirmish on a ridge at Roodikop near Dewetsdorp, along with the 9th Lancers and 14th Hussars. The latter regiments suffered heavy casualties and the 7th Dragoons lost one man. On 27 April they covered an infantry attack. They became separated from the infantry and came under fire from a force of 1,200 Boers so they dismounted and returned fire as best they

Captain G. Langworthy leading 'B' Squadron across Parys Drift. Copyright © Royal Dragoon Guards Collection, York Army Museum

could with their carbines. Dickson had to order a withdrawal at dusk and the 7th retired under fire.

On 10 May when they were heading for Kroonstadt, the regiment, along with the 8th Hussars, had what was now becoming a rare experience for cavalry: a full-blooded mounted charge, swords whirling above heads as they rode at a force of about three hundred Boer riflemen who had ridden out into the open. The charge had to be cut short, however. Luckily for them, they spotted a ravine running across their path which would have been fatal if they had all tumbled into it but they managed to turn away in time. It had been a trick to lure the two regiments on but the casualties were few compared to what might have been.

The conditions were beginning to take their toll on the horses. Many of the original ones brought from England had been lost. Remounts, also shipped out were put to service before they had recovered from the sea voyage, and the heat and carrying heavy loads for up to thirty miles a day was exhausting them. Often the men had no access to their transport as well, simply having what they could carry on their horses. (The 'transport' is a caravan of wagons pulled by mules or oxen which contains most of the supplies and can only move at slow pace, particularly across rough ground.)

The 4th Brigade of which they were part continued to advance, and for the most part met little resistance as the Boer fighters fell away against superior odds. Confidence of an imminent victory began to grow amongst the British. This was shaken on 28 May when they came under heavy attack which continued on 29 as they closed in on Johannesburg. On 30 May they passed near to Witwatersrand, the site of the gold mines which had been one of the triggers for the war. They were warmly welcomed by the mine owners and managers because the Boers had threatened to destroy the mining machinery rather than let it fall into British hands. On 31 May Johannesburg surrendered to the British. The sense that the war would soon be over began to grow. As British troops moved the few miles north to the Transvaal capital of Pretoria, they encountered some resistance, but learned later that this was a holding strategy designed to enable the Boers to retreat from their capital. They must have done this with heavy heart, but realised that to defend it would have come at too high a price and eventually would have ended in defeat, such was the size of the British military force by that time. On 7 June, negotiations began between the British and the Boers. The British demanded unconditional surrender but this was unacceptable to the Boers and the war, instead of ending, entered its second, guerrilla, phase. The Boers knew they could not defeat the British in conventional warfare, so adapted the strategy of well chosen attacks, both large and small against an enemy constantly in need of supplies and reinforcements.

Almost straight away, on 11 June, the battle of Diamond Hill began. This was George's most challenging experience of combat to date. At dawn, the cavalry division he was in marched out of their camp, under orders to attack the right flank of the

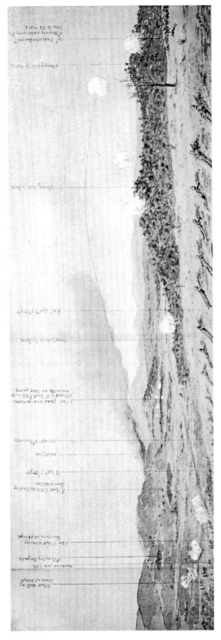

From a sketch made at the time of the Battle of Diamond Hill, from Kameelfontein looking northeast, showing the part taken in the battle by General French's Cavalry Division, on the left flank. 11–12 June 1900. By Major B. R. Dietz. Copyright © Royal Dragoon Guards Collection, York Army Museum

George relaxing. Courtesy of Remi Fernandez Campoy

George's dog Toby tangles with a monkey. Courtesy of Remi Fernandez Campoy

line the Boers were holding about 15 miles from Pretoria. By
8.30 a.m. George's squadron was in a position in open country
providing supporting fire from their ineffective carbines with
only sporadic patches of grass for cover. They were pinned in
this position for over fifty hours. Any attempt to move provoked
a hail of fire from the Boers occupying a small hill only 800
metres away. The British did not have sufficient numbers to drive
back the Boers until other Cavalry Brigades miles away to their
right began to force them to retreat. This battle signalled the
end of set-piece engagements in the war. This attack and retreat
method of warfare would soon be the favoured tactic of the
Boers as a response to the superior numbers of the British. That
afternoon, General French assembled the commanding Officers
and Squadron Commanders, including George, to congratulate
them on their skill under sustained heavy fire. British casualties
were minimal, but the experience had a very demoralising effect.
Four weeks of welcome rest were to follow.

George next saw close action in late July when they had moved
southeast of Pretoria and he was ordered to dislodge a group of
Boers firing on the British with a pom-pom. This was a new kind
of weapon, which worked like a machine gun but fired one-pound
shells. The Boers often used them in 'shoot and scoot' missions,
firing 30–50 shells then changing position. George dismounted his
men to lead them up a ridge and the squadron's horses suffered
greatly under fire from the pom-pom as he achieved his objective.
August and September were occupied with moving east to achieve
strategic objectives. The British cavalry were re-organised and
dispersed to separate mobile columns to combat the fragmented
way of fighting. They were issued with new rifles, the infantry
pattern Lee-Enfield .303 calibre. The Lee Enfield carbines that they
had first been issued with were said to be on average 180–200 yards
undersighted (a 'carbine' is a short rifle, generally preferred when
riding horseback). The new rifles were capable of being fitted with
a bayonet so swords were dispensed with. Their tasks involved the

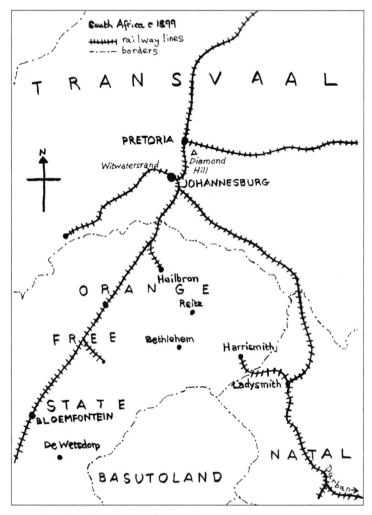

Map of significant places in George's experience in S. Africa. © Gill Shapton

Officers of 'O' battery and 7th Dragoons (George seated first right). Copyright © Royal Dragoon Guards Collection, York Army Museum.

destruction of farms in an effort to cut off the Boer's food supply, and the rounding up of Boer civilians suspected of aiding the fighters. In 1901 they spent much of their time chasing the elusive Christiaan De Wet and his commandos.

George was one of seven officers of his regiment mentioned as rendering special and meritorious service by Lord Roberts in his final despatch of September 1900 before handing over command of British Forces to Lord Kitchener. After taking part in the major advance to the east, witnessing sporadic attacks, George returned to the area of Johannesburg, but by Christmas 1900 found himself back down in Cape Colony because a large Boer force had now entered the territory. Meanwhile, under Lord Kitchener the British strategy now included burning any farms considered to be of strategic or tactical value to the Boers and transporting displaced women and children to concentration camps. In addition, troops were instructed to round up all livestock and transport them with them to deprive the Boers of their use.

The terrain in Cape Colony was very different to Transvaal which had been open and rough. Here was a lot more mountainous and troops often moved around in smaller units, engaged in 'cat and mouse' tactics with the Boers. George and his men now had a full complement of fit horses and they were able to travel much more quickly. The troops were now organised into columns consisting of cavalry, infantry and artillery and were constantly on the move. A calculation was made that over nine days in late February/early March 1901 the baggage wagons of the column George was in had travelled 223 miles, that is over twenty-four miles a day. Gradually they had moved back towards Transvaal and were in the north-east of the Orange Free State.

By now George's squadron, 'B' squadron, had earned the nickname the 'Busy Bees' and they reinforced that over a period of five days in May. George and his squadron, together with fifty yeomen were detailed to escort a General who had

George at Harrismith. Courtesy of Remi Fernandez Campoy

been taken ill to the town of Heilbron for medical treatment. Marching through the night of 5 May, at daybreak, through thick mist, they heard the lowing of cattle and shouting of drivers. Suspecting the cause, George sent forward a troop which surprised a 'laager' (a defensive encampment encircled by wagons) on a farm called Oploop and captured six ox-wagons and six Cape carts full of women, children and armed men, some of whom escaped. A second laager was discovered and rushed at a farm called Kaalfontein and included twelve wagons, ten Cape carts and seven armed men. In addition they had captured about 500 head of cattle, some thirty horses and a quantity of

A Blockhouse. Copyright © Royal Dragoon Guards Collection, York Army Museum

ammunition. George's opportunism served him well, because as they approached Heilbron they spotted armed Boers who probably did not fire on them for fear of hurting their own people held captive by George's men. During the ensuing months, the work there was absolutely incessant, often going on night and day. Apart from repeated captures of wagons, livestock and men, women and children, the column George was in attacked the town of Reitz in the early hours of 11 July and captured all but one member of the government of the ex-president of Orange Free Colony. The exception was the ex-president himself, Steyn, who managed to escape on horseback. Two days later the prisoners were taken to Pretoria to be questioned by Lord Kitchener.

On 30 September, most of the column George was in was ordered to Zululand. George headed one of the details left behind at Harrismith, which was where the column had arrived on 25 September. Harrismith is a town in the Orange Free State fifty miles northwest of Ladysmith. The British had occupied it in August 1900. The town was at one end of a line of 134 blockhouses to Bethlehem and another of sixteen to the Oliver's Hoek Pass. A blockhouse is a small fortification designed as a defensive strong point. These blockhouses played a vital role in the protection of the railway lines and bridges that were key to the British military supply lines. Harrismith was also a location for both white and black concentration camps.

> During the absence of the Regiment in Zululand the details left behind had some sharp fighting. One night expedition was particularly exciting. The details under Captain Langworthy were ordered to join the KDG (King's Dragoon Guards) and some 3rd DG the whole under General Broadwood to make a night march on a strong position held by the Boers called Witze's Hook. We started out, the KDG doing advanced guard and nothing happened till about midnight when a shot rang out. This shot accounted for the life of a most gallant officer, Major Quicke KDG who was killed by an old Boer in rounding up a farm. Shortly after the Boers started to snipe at the column and a stray bullet hit Captain Langworthy wounding him severely in the thigh. This was very bad luck as the range must have been about 2,000 yards as the 7th Dragoon Guards were towards the rear of the column.

These are the words describing George's last action in South Africa as recounted in a series of reminiscences of the war published in the regiment's journal, the *Black Horse Gazette* from 1906 to 1909. George left South Africa from Durban on 2 December on board the Royal Mail Ship *Tagus* employed as a troopship. The ship carried four hundred soldiers, sick and well, and three nursing sisters and was due in Southampton three days before Christmas. During the voyage back to England, George will have had plenty of time to reflect on his 'very bad luck'. There is no reason to assume that he could not continue his career in the army, though probably in a less active role, perhaps even limited to the UK. His days winning horse races in the regiment were over, maybe his hunting days too. They had brought him so much enjoyment and plenty of prestige among officers and men. The brigade had even found time to put on races in rest periods during the campaign. Now all that was over. But he had a wife waiting for him at home and they could start married life in earnest after a honeymoon period between the ceremony and his departure for Cape Town.

Two weeks after George's injury, Annie's sister Frances Douie gave birth to what would be her last child and called her Decima Langworthy Douie. Perhaps she wanted to pay tribute to her brother-in-law or raise the spirits of the young couple as they faced an uncertain future.

Being reunited with her husband, albeit that he was wounded, must have been the best Christmas present Annie could have had. Given that his wound was severe George must have spent a considerable time convalescing in the UK. They will have soon begun planning their future life together. Annie by now had experienced at least four English winters and if her health was not good, as reported by those who later knew her in Spain, then the quest would be on to find a place with a climate that would be kind to her and to a severely wounded soldier. In March 1903 George was promoted to the rank of major. In May he was placed on temporary half pay on account of his continuing ill health. In November he retired and was placed on retired pay. On the twenty-third of that month, he and Annie boarded the RMS *Omrah* at Plymouth. bound for Gibraltar. Less than a week before they sailed Annie signed her original will in Falmouth. The last minute will-writing may give us an indication of the state of Annie's health.

CHAPTER NINE
Málaga and Santa Clara

Here is a spot which seems designed by nature to be the health resort of Europe; a perfect climate absolutely faultless for eight months of the year; a thermometer which does not vary five degrees Farenheit [*sic*] month in month out; an inexhaustible supply of the purest water; fruit and vegetables in lavish abundance; fish of all varieties and great excellence; direct communications with England, France and Italy by sea, and railway connections of course . . . It lies in a rich valley about ten miles in extent, with mountains on three sides, which shelter it from all the cold winds,

Málaga port. See http://www.malagahistoria.com

while on the south it is open to the sea. The near hills are green
with verdure, while red and yellow, brown and gray [*sic*] mix in the
coloring of the sterile masses of rock that rise beyond them into,
rough, lofty outlines; and beyond them again are the snow-white
distant mountains The sunshine is absolutely unfailing; an average
of thirty nine days of rainfall a year makes the dryness of the air
phenomenal. You find you must have had a sore throat all your life
without knowing it; breathing is a revelation; digestion takes care
of itself. The atmosphere is transparent, the sea and the sky of a
marvellous blue; the soil is generous like the people; it looks like
rocks and rubbish, but out of it grows tropical vegetation without
any apparent moisture. Palm, banana, orange, eucalyptus, and
cypress trees fill the gardens, olive and almond orchards cover the
hills. All sorts of amiable flowers which we cultivate at home, such
as periwinkle, carnations, oxalis, and sweet alyssum wander over
the rocks wild. The rose, with all its train of sweet summer flowers,
walks through the entire year in rich abundance.

It is easy to imagine a newly married Annie Langworthy
reading these words while shivering through an English winter
at her father's house in Oxford and wondering if this would be
a good place for her and her husband to make a home once he
returned from the war in South Africa. They are the words of
Miriam Coles Harris, an American novelist who, after the death
of her husband in 1892, spent most of her time in Europe. In
1898 her account of a stay in Málaga called *A Corner of Spain* was
published. Harris went on to compare Málaga with the French
Riviera, a popular choice for wealthy north Europeans at the
time: 'the Riviera is more or less damp in all parts; the chill that
falls at sunset is felt keenly, and there is a suspicion of malaria
always.' In Málaga by contrast:

The transition from day to night brings no shock and there is
absolutely no malaria. The death-rate is very low, even under the

evil conditions of squalor and starvation in which the lower class live. If Málaga could be brought up to the standard of the Riviera towns, it could not fail of popularity. Spain is not so worn out a field for the idle, and for the ill there is but one attraction, and that is health, here more surely found than there. A corporal's guard of dull English people yearly come here with their invalids and take them home cured, but they do not spread the matter, having no interest in the enlargement of Málaga's borders, and not being by nature of a proselytising turn.

If it is true that Annie had poor health, then she would not have welcomed the prospect of many more English winters. She had spent much of her time growing up in the heat of India, and Málaga is bound to have seemed very attractive with the bonus of not having the extremes of the Indian climate. The profound poverty of the poor in Spain is something commented on by other foreign writers, but a daughter of the Raj will not have been put off by such reports considering the condition of most of the native population of India at that time.

When George came back from the war badly wounded it will have, at some point, become clear that his active military career was over. He would have his military pension, and more importantly his portfolio of investments, and one of the attractions of Málaga as compared to, say, the French Riviera, was the cost of living. As Harris informed her readers:

> Living here, of course, is cheap as compared with America or France. The rent of a villa on the Caleta or an apartment on the Alameda would probably be much less than the corresponding quarters in any winter resort in Europe . . . Servants' wages are very low; the servants, however, as a rule are not very good. The food is cheap, the meat ought to be nothing, it is so poor, but no doubt it has a nominal price. The vegetables and fruit and fish, as I said, are fit for a prince's table and so are the wines.

As in India where Annie will have spent most of her time in the company of other English people, Harris informs us that 'The society in a Spanish city uncontaminated by tourists is worth studying. There are enough English settled here to take off the dreariness of absolute isolation.' It is estimated that there were about four hundred British residents in Málaga by about 1900. The total population was about 100,000, about one-sixth of the population of Manchester but twice the size of Oxford. This ex-pat population of Málaga so sniffily acknowledged by Harris will have been an added attraction for the 'enterprising' English who might choose to visit to enjoy the winter climate.

The Britons in Málaga were not just retirees but also economically active. Nineteenth century Spain was on the receiving end of what has been called British 'soft imperialism'. Spain became politically and economically weaker throughout the nineteenth century, losing its large colonies in South and Central America just as Britain's successful industrial revolution led to a demand for raw materials, the capital to invest in them and a command of the seas to ensure their safe passage both from its Empire but also from 'informal colonies'. Spain became one of these 'informal colonies': sovereign states with less developed economies. Spain had seen limited, patchy industrial progress but remained a largely agricultural society, almost feudal in places with much potentially productive land unused. To achieve this 'soft imperialism' the British government intervened effectively in Spain's internal affairs to ensure a government favourable to British interests. Spain itself was identified as a lucrative commercial market, especially for the Manchester textile industry from the 1830s onwards. For a variety of reasons linked to Spain's economic and political weakness and Britain's commercial and military strength, Britain had a dominant economic and political role in the country. A notable area of British investment in Andalucía was the mining of minerals. The Royal Mines of Rio Tinto were sold to a British-led consortium at a price below their worth. These mines contained the largest deposits of pyrites in the world and were the world's main source of copper and sulphur for forty years once the new owners had developed efficient extraction practices. The profits were spectacular. The company, still called Rio Tinto, is now Anglo-Australian and one of the world's largest metals and mining corporations. From the 1870s some 13 per cent of all British investment in Europe went to Spain, especially mining.

British interference in Spain preceded this nineteenth century economic dominance. At one point Spain was England's number one enemy. Every English schoolchild was taught that Spain had sent an Armada against England in 1588 and lost. At the time of the loss of the Armada, Spain was in fact a global power with an empire consisting of Latin America (except Brazil), parts of what is now the United States of America, the East Indies, including the Phillipines, and parts of Europe including the greater part of Italy, some parts of modern France and Germany and the area which is now Belgium, the Netherlands and Luxembourg. Its navy commanded the Atlantic and Pacific oceans and most of the Mediterranean. Wealth poured into the country especially from the gold and silver mines of Mexico and Bolivia. However, the success which pre-dated the Empire also left a debilitating legacy: after 1492 when Ferdinand and Isabel celebrated the reconquest of the country from the Moors and its re-Christianisation, most Moors and Jews were expelled. Much expertise in commerce, industry and agriculture was lost to Spain, but the incoming colonial wealth removed the motivation to replace that knowledge amongst the rich and educated part of the population.

The decline of the seventeenth century was reversed to some extent in the eighteenth, but not until after the War of Spanish Succession which lasted from 1701 to 1714. Although it was fought to determine who should sit on the Spanish throne it was a European war, involving several countries including

Britain. In the Treaty of Utrecht at the end of the war, Spain was forced to give up its European possessions. This included ceding Gibraltar, which was captured by an Anglo-Dutch force in 1704, to Britain in perpetuity. By the middle of the century the ideals of the Enlightenment were entering the country but the Catholic Church set itself resolutely against these new ideas of reason and scientific progress The desire of the Church to retain its dominant role in Spanish society characterised the country well beyond then, and arguably up to and after the Civil War of 1936–9. Conflict revisited the country when Napoleon invaded in 1808. After his final defeat on the Iberian Peninsula in 1814, a long period of political instability ensued including three internal wars between 1833 and 1876 (the Carlist Wars) which reflected the struggle between liberal and reactionary Spain seen in the previous century. In 1898 Spain lost its last colonies: the Phillipines, Puerto Rico and Cuba. This was known in the country as 'El Desastre' ('The Disaster').

A century of political and economic decline had ended in national humiliation but at least there had been no war on Spanish soil for a quarter of a century, so it was becoming more attractive to other Europeans as an affordable place to visit or settle, especially south coast destinations like Málaga where the proximity of Gibraltar offered an assurance of safety. Its value as an accessible route back to Britain if needed would have been a consideration in the mind of anyone considering settling in southern Spain at that time. Regardless of the attraction of Spain, George and Annie did not want to sever ties with England. They travelled back there, and family and friends visited during their time together in Andalucía. The earliest return visit I have located is that George was on the guest list for a regimental banquet in London in October 1904.

Our American visitor Harris had strong views about Gibraltar, 'the Rock'. Although she delighted in its natural features, she was not overly impressed by its human inhabitants and their creations: 'one feels a certain bewilderment in straying about in streets bearing all sorts of English names, and swarming with all sorts of foreign people'. She learned that it was not a popular posting with the British army: 'the officers loath [*sic*] it, and with the men it is equally unpopular . . . The crack regiments are not sent here, I am told, and the flavour of life is insipid in consequence.' Nevertheless her description of the social life contains echoes of British India:

> The Hunting Club has good sport . . . The meets of course are all in Spain . . . but the sport is said to be excellent . . . There are tennis, and badminton, and polo, and cricket, and rowing clubs, and two or three theatres . . . the governor has to give two balls a year . . . there are subscription dances, and masquerades, and dinners, and teas *ad nauseam* . . . But Gibraltar . . . is a beastly bore, a dismal hole, to the officers stationed here.

Her description matches many views of colonial life in India but the potential rewards of the Raj made any social drawbacks a price worth paying for many enterprising British.

Underneath this veneer of British respectability a flourishing trade in smuggling operated from Gibraltar. Although the Rock had begun life under British rule as a military post, the civilian population gradually grew, and with it, both legal and illegal trade with Spain. In the first half of the nineteenth century one of the principal commodities smuggled was textiles, especially from Manchester. It is in the nature of smuggling that it is impossible to know if any goods from the Greengate Mills of Langworthy Bros. & Co. ever passed this way. The practice was hardly clandestine, however. The merchants of Gibraltar, and the British government itself, felt no responsibility for checking the flow of tariff-free goods into Spain. In 1841 the Foreign Secretary, Lord Palmerston declared:

> If the Spanish government want to put a stop to that smuggling which Her Majesty's government are well aware is carried on to a great extent through Gibraltar into Spain, the only effectual way . . . is by a revision of the Spanish tariff for the purpose of placing it in harmony with the wants and wishes of the Spanish nation and in accordance with the commercial spirit of the age.

In other words it is Spain's fault for not agreeing to fair trade. In some cases Spanish smugglers would have Gibraltarians register vessels in their name so that if the vessels were pursued by the Spanish authorities they were entitled to protection from British forces. The scale of the smuggling was considerable. Until the middle of the nineteenth century, more goods were officially imported to Gibraltar than to the whole of Spain. By the end of the century tobacco was the main item of contraband, smuggled in large quantities but also by individual Spaniards who also hid it on dogs, donkeys, horses and even turkeys in ingenious ways.

All this may have been unknown to Harris who had arrived at Gibraltar from New York on board the ship she calls 'the Kaiser'. This was the SS *Kaiser Wilhelm de Grosse* which made its maiden voyage in September 1897. The ship, owned by Norddeutscher Lloyd, is considered the first 'superliner', the fastest and latest in ocean-going luxury at the time, though sadly Harris's voyage was marred by a storm lasting 'six dreadful days'. More perils awaited her and her companion: from Gibraltar she had to travel to Algeciras by boat, first a rowboat to take her to a tug which carried her to Algeciras. While she was waiting for the rowboat 'it began to rain furiously . . . I have never been exposed to so heavy a rain, and after we got outside the mole the waves were high.' Then they had to 'bob up and down beside the little steam tug, waiting for a favourable wave to precipitate us on board her; and why our luggage was not spilled over into the sea . . . I do not know.'

The twenty-first century reader might wonder why this was all necessary as Gibraltar is physically part of the Spanish mainland and a good road leads from there to Málaga. There would have been three options in 1898 for getting from Gibraltar to Málaga. A road of sorts would have existed but would have been unmetalled and very poor. There was a history of bandits operating in Andalucía though they were less likely to attack on the coast road than in the mountains. Boats would ply between Gibraltar and Málaga, many probably owned by smugglers, but Harris undertook the next stage of the journey by rail via Bobadilla, about seventy kilometres north of Málaga where the line connected with the line which ran from Málaga northwards. This is the journey that George and Annie may well have undertaken when they first arrived in Gibraltar in 1903, though as a British military officer George may have been able to arrange land transfer to the train from Algeciras rather than risk the perils of Harris's 'little steam tug'.

Harris's spirits were much lifted by the rail journey:

> From nine, when we left terraced and picturesque Algeciras, till twilight settled down over the land as we drew near Málaga there was not a moment when we were willing to turn from the windows of the carriage and to forego the landscape . . . You go from one range of sierras to another; you have scarcely subdued your raptures over one wild gorge than you come upon another cleft mountain and tumbling cascade which obliterates the first. Crags crowned with Moorish ruins, villages climbing up green hillsides, rugged mountains and sterile plains, paint each other out with rapid brush. Orchards of gray-green olives, and of pale pink almond blossoms, groves of eucalyptus, sentinels of cypress, palm, banana and cork trees.

Annie's spirits might also have been high if they made the same rail journey at the end of November 1903. Climate apart, Málaga, viewed in the patchwork of Spain's uneven social and industrial development, was a bright spot. In the nineteenth century it had become an industrial centre with textile factories,

The Roe family home in Lahore. Courtesy of the University of Queensland, Hume Collection, Firth Library.

George at the Villa in Málaga. Courtesy of Remi Fernandez Campoy.

sugar and steel mills and shipyards which is why a prosperous expatriate community of north Europeans already existed when George and his wife arrived there. George's purchase of the land in Torremolinos in 1905 suggests that part of the couple's plan was to own a large property with its own grounds. A surviving photograph of Annie's family home in Lahore shows a quite palatial building. We can only speculate on the extent of the grounds but they are likely to have been considerable.

Although the purchase of El Castillo and Santa Clara was completed in 1905 George's regimental gazette for January 1906 reports that he was living at the Villa Estella in Málaga. It is likely that the couple were still resident in Málaga then because it will have taken some time to make the property at Torremolinos habitable.

This report of George's whereabouts was in the January 1906 edition of the *Black Horse Gazette*, the first edition to be issued for over six years. Production had ceased because of the regiment's involvement in war in South Africa. Coincidentally, the final edition in 1899 had carried news of George and Annie's marriage. As the *Gazette* put it: 'Many congratulations to Captain Langworthy on his marriage; but at the same time, hearty condolences to his brother officers. Another good bachelor lost to the mess! At the present rate of engagements we shall be able to do without a mess at all in a year or two.'

Once settled in Málaga, George and Annie hired Sebastián Salas as their gardener and sometime chauffeur and his fiancée Carmen Jiménez as cook and maid to Annie. It was Sebastián who first told them about 'El Castillo', an abandoned fort along the coast to the west in the fishing village of Torremolinos They learned that there were two adjacent properties: El Castillo, a former fort, and Santa Clara, a farmhouse, both in the possession of one man, Don Liborio García, a former mayor of Málaga. The estate consisted of a house on the Santa Clara component of 231 square metres plus a smaller building of 40 square metres, and the building known as the Castillo covering 829 metres. The total estate amounted to 134.2 hectares (330 acres) surrounded by walls, railings and stone benches, remnants of water ponds and a service road. The buildings required massive renovation, but there was an ample water supply meaning that the surrounding land could be developed into a lush garden.

The site of the fort will have impressed them from the first. The land on which the fort was built was known as the Punta de (Point of) Torremolinos and thrust forward into the

Santa Clara from La Carihuela beach. This image shows a stairway down to the beach added later. Courtesy of Remi Fernandez Campoy

blue Mediterranean with beautiful beaches to either side, La Carihuela to the south and El Bajondillo to the north. The *punta* was formed of travertine, a type of sedimentary limestone created by deposits from ground and surface water springs. It often has a fibrous appearance, as it does on the *punta*, something which can be seen to this day despite the extensive degree of modern building. The plentiful supply of fresh water came from the natural springs which had helped create the *punta* and which had facilitated the construction of *molinos* (mills) centuries earlier.

The mills were used for grinding corn, but also, it is believed, for milling lentils, salt and iron ore. It is estimated that the Moors who occupied that area before the Christian reconquest of Spain in the late fifteenth century had established eighteen mills, the waters from seventeen of which went on to irrigate fields and orchards. The channel which delivered this water began at the Molino de las Incas which can still be seen in the botanical gardens of Torremolinos. To guard this valuable agricultural resource, the Moors constructed a *torre de vigia* (watchtower) in about 1300. Hence the name the Spanish gave the settlement when the Málaga coastal area was captured from the Moors in 1487: Torre de los Molinos – Tower of the Mills.

Moving forward to the eighteenth century, the concern about the amount of smuggling and the increasing presence of pirates on the coast, led to the creation of the post of captain-general of the coast with the intention of fortifying the whole coastline, with some sort of control centre to monitor every known inlet and anchorage. (Incidentally, the first invasion of Torremolinos by the English was not in the 1960s but in 1704 after England had entered the War of Spanish Succession in a Grand Alliance against the Spanish and French. Admiral George Rooke wanted to exchange prisoners and take on water from the springs of Torremolinos but his request was refused and he sent ashore 2,000 soldiers who looted stocks of grain and livestock as well as setting fire to the mills.)

At Torremolinos, apart from the gently shelving beaches where boats could easily land, the travertine limestone meant that the area offered a number of caves ideal for smuggling expeditions. In 1769 the *castillo* that George eventually bought was completed, replacing an earlier, ineffective fortification. The fort was intended not only to police the immediate area, but to be a strategic component of the defence of the Bay of Málaga, offering excellent visibility because of its raised position and of course, an uninterrupted line of fire in the event of attack. The

Main house under reconstruction. Courtesy of Remi Fernandez Campoy

The completed house showing the wide veranda reminiscent of the Indian colonial style. Courtesy of Remi Fernandez Campoy

Napoleonic Wars saw the partial destruction of this and other coastal fortifications. The French, for their part, wanted to destroy any artillery capability. The British, when they signed the alliance with Spain against Napoleon, wanted to see the end of the ring of fortifications to ensure their regional naval superiority. Once Spain was able to restore these defences, improvements in artillery meant less of them were needed, but the strategic importance of the fort at Torremolinos was recognised and it was reinstated, this time as a barracks for carabineers in 1830. In the second half of the nineteenth century the site ceased to serve that function and passed into private hands as the State tried to realise funds from redundant assets to reduce the national debt.

George officially became the owner of both properties on 22 May 1905 having paid the sum of 72,500 pesetas, approximately £2,500, a small proportion of his wealth. One of the first changes he made was to order the re-construction of the house, to be their home on the 'Santa Clara' part of the property. The house was re-built to a design that echoed the British colonial style in India, with wide verandas to offer plenty of shade from the sun. At the same time work began on the grounds of the two combined properties to create areas for the cultivation of crops and flowers including on the land to the seaward side of the barracks. Originally the 'cuartel' (barracks) was not renovated. It was to serve as stables and storage for agricultural and horticultural equipment.

Once the main house had been built, George and Annie moved in, deciding finally that the name of their new home would be 'Santa Clara'.

They took with them Sebastián and Carmen, who married soon after. Before long they hired two gardeners, brothers called Frasquito and Pepe, who did not live in. Work continued on the buildings and grounds right up to 1912, with a tennis court being one of the last things to be created. George also hired a local boatman, Antonio Campoy, to assist him with a boat he had bought for him and Annie to sail along the coast from time to time.

George's boat. Courtesy of Remi Fernandez Campoy.

Planting in front of the main house. Courtesy of Remi Fernandez Campoy.

Planting in front of the main house. Courtesy of Remi Fernandez Campoy.

Developed land around cuartel. Courtesy of Remi Fernandez Campoy.

George (*second left*) poses with a hunting party. Courtesy of Remi Fernandez Campoy.

Staff ready the dogs for an expedition. Courtesy of Remi Fernandez Campoy.

Remi Fernandez Campoy, the daughter of Antonio Campoy's niece, lived on the estate from her birth in 1946 until 1965 and vividly recalls the rich variety of flowers, fruits and vegetables that were grown in the grounds:

The varieties of flowers included wisteria, *celestinas*, honeysuckle, gardenias, night jasmine, mock orange, geraniums, *gitanillas*, gladioli, chrysanthemum, carnations, wallflowers, cosmos, phlox, daisies and a plethora of roses – tree varieties, bushes, climbers, miniatures.

The trees included fig, medlar, custard apple, orange, lemon, pear, apricot, peach, eucalyptus, pines and palms. Remi remembers that owls shared their living quarters with sparrows in the palm trees and that a custard apple tree supported a swing. She also recalls that George loved jam made from the medlar fruit.

The vegetables grown in the grounds included potatoes, sweet potatoes, tomatoes and peppers and many more, as well as vines.

Some of what they grew will have reminded George and Annie of the hill stations in India such as Simla, the summer capital of

Waiting to shoot.
Courtesy of Remi Fernandez Campoy.

A picnic in woods. Courtesy of Remi
Fernandez Campoy.

British India. The same kinds of flowers that thrived there could
flourish in the Mediterranean climate. Apart from the flowers, fruit
and vegetables, pigs and chickens were also reared on the estate.
Ducks enjoyed the pleasure of an ornamental lake.

Dogs, especially Jack Russells, were constant companions of
the couple. The notable exception from surviving photographs of
the period is horses. As an ex-cavalryman, surrounded by wild and
varied country, riding and hunting on horseback would have been
an attractive proposition both for George and many of his visitors.
The absence of horses from the surviving photographs suggests
that the wound George sustained in the Boer War had brought
his riding days to an end. However other hunting activities clearly
remained an option.

Jack Russells had been bred as a hunting dog since the middle of
the nineteenth century. Initially bred for foxhunting they proved to
be adaptable and implacable hunters. The animals were also clearly
seen as pets, and George created a pet cemetery in the grounds.

Expeditions into the countryside were not just for hunting but
picnics too.

Modes of transport varied. One day the latest in motoring
technology, another day tradition prevails.

Annie, George and a friend with some of their dogs. Courtesy of Remi Fernandez Campoy.

Annie and her sister on a donkey ride. Courtesy of Remi Fernandez Campoy.

Receiving guests at Santa Clara. Courtesy of Remi Fernandez Campoy.

Annie (*seated*) and George, possibly with relatives. Courtesy of Remi Fernandez Campoy.

A motor car in difficulty. Courtesy of Remi Fernandez Campoy.

The Star, on the left, and the De Dion-Bouton. Courtesy of Remi Fernandez Campoy.

A send-off from the village children. Courtesy of Remi Fernandez Campoy.

There were occasions when tradition may have been preferable to modernity.

Two cars feature in photographs from the time, a Star, manufactured in Wolverhampton and a De Dion-Bouton manufactured in Puteaux on the outskirts of Paris.

While Santa Clara afforded them the earthly paradise they had sought, George and Annie continued to maintain an active social life, visiting the friends they had made in Málaga since their arrival in 1903.

As the refurbishment of the house progressed they were better able to receive local guests and visitors from England, including family.

They also made trips to England every year or two. In 1906 in London, Annie added a codicil to the will she had written in 1903. In the codicil she left all the property in Spain to which she might have been entitled to Florence Honor Langworthy. This is George's only surviving cousin, the spinster sister of the infamous EML who had brought such shame on the family name. We can assume they felt concern for Florence's future.

In 1908 there was a further trip to England. The first year that the 20-hp Star car was manufactured was 1908, and one purpose of the trip might have been to road-test and buy the car. George and Annie drove through France in the summer of 1909 in the Star. George wrote up the drive through France in an article for the *Black Horse Gazette* published the following summer. It is reproduced in full as an appendix as it is the only known example of George's own writing.

They were perhaps in England for Christmas 1910. Both still had relatives in the south of England and in Manchester They sailed for Gibraltar in January 1911, but George, at least, must have been back later in the year because he was at a regimental dinner in London in June 1911.

Through all the comings and goings, work on the house and grounds continued.

Enjoying tea on the verandah. Courtesy of Remi Fernandez Campoy.

Enjoying tea on the verandah. Courtesy of Remi Fernandez Campoy.

A shady corner with friend and dogs. Courtesy of Remi Fernandez Campoy.

The tennis court. Courtesy of Carlos Beautell.

Annie. Courtesy of Remi
Fernandez Campoy.

Annie in mantilla.
Courtesy of Remi Fernandez Campoy.

They could enjoy tea in the shade of the deep veranda.

Or relax in a shady corner with friends and dogs.

George had sheltered viewpoints ('miradores') constructed for enjoying the sight of the Mediterranean.

He loved a game of tennis and it is said that the creation of the tennis court in 1912 was perhaps the final touch.

Only months later all of George's plans received the cruellest blow. On 28 January 2013, Annie died from pneumonia at the age of forty. The pain of the bullet tearing into his flesh in South Africa little more than a decade earlier will have felt like nothing compared to the agony George felt on the loss of Annie, the loss of the life they had built together under the Spanish sun, a life more beautiful than they could have dreamed of that winter's day in London in 1899 when they made their vows together. As George laid his wife's body to rest in the English Cemetery in Málaga it would be surprising if his grief was not mingled with despair. Not once, but twice had fate robbed him of the life he

IN LOVING MEMORY
OF
ANNIE MARGARET,
THE DEARLY LOVED WIFE OF
MAJOR GEORGE LANGWORTHY
OF SANTA CLARA, TORREMOLINOS,
WHO PEACEFULLY PASSED AWAY
28TH JANUARY 1913
ONE FAITH, ONE HOPE, ONE SPIRIT,
IN HIM WE LIVE UNITED STILL.

Inscription on Annie's grave. © Mike Shapton.

had chosen. First that stray bullet in the South African night had robbed him of his career, the cavalry life he loved. But he had married before it had struck and now he and his bride had found a place, a life, which was good, which could ward off threats to Annie's delicate health, which brought peace and beauty after the horror of war. But no, it was not to be, and as Annie's body was lowered into its last resting place George must have felt he was staring into an abyss. Could he bear to live in this Paradise they had created together? Could he enjoy the Spanish warmth without Annie beside him? Could he cope with the well-intentioned sympathy of the friends they had made here, who now stood around him at the graveside? He did not rush into any decisions and spent some time in England that summer, perhaps seeing to Annie's affairs, and returned to Santa Clara in August. George could have given up Spain at that point. He could have arranged for Annie to be buried in England and found himself a place to live. He still had brothers and sisters living in various parts of England. It must have been painful for him to return

George in his First World War major's uniform. Courtesy of Remi Fernandez Campoy.

to Santa Clara that August and be surrounded by everything he
and Annie had created, but he must have felt this was their home,
their only real home together, and he would always be nearer to
her here.

The following year international events were again going to
shape the future course of George's life. In August 1914, Britain

and Germany went to war. Like many retired soldiers, George will have wanted to help the war effort and he set sail for England at the first opportunity. There was a widely held belief that the war would be over by Christmas 1914, so he probably did not expect to be away for long. George's old regiment fought in the war. It was now under the command of Lt. Col. H. A Lempriere whose signature appeared on Georges' marriage certificate, and was probably his best man. He was the first officer of the regiment to be killed in the Great War, dying on 21 December 1914.

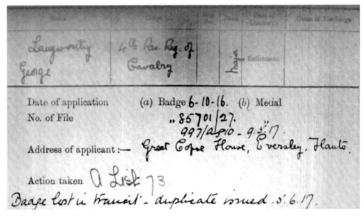

Image of George's silver badge award. See https://www.findmypast.co.uk/

As a retired officer of the 7th Dragoons, Major George Langworthy, now aged forty-nine, did not see active service but served in the 4th Reserve Regiment of Cavalry stationed at Tidworth Barracks in Wiltshire. The regiment was one of several reserves formed in August 1914. It trained new recruits for the 4th and 7th Dragoon Guards, Warwickshire Yeomanry, Gloucestershire Yeomanry and Worcestershire Yeomanry.

The war in South Africa had taught the British Cavalry some painful lessons. For cavalry to survive they had to change tactics and the emphasis was now on dismounted firepower and cavalry charges that were supported by covering fire. George will have experienced this change of tactics while in South Africa, so his knowledge would have been invaluable. To support this change in policy, cavalrymen were now required to do two hours rifle or sword practice a day. The resulting reforms helped shape the cavalry's contribution to the war and all regiments were armed with machine guns and equipped with entrenching tools.

None of the Reserve Cavalry Regiments saw action in the main theatres of the war, though four (not including George's) saw combat in the 1916 Easter Rising in Dublin, where the commanding officer was Brigadier General William Lowe, George's former commanding officer in the war in South Africa.

By 1916, George himself was suffering ill health and he was formally discharged from the army in September of that year.

In November, he set sail on a ship bound for Spain with his sister Sarah, the widow of a baronet, William Wiseman, who had died in 1893. Interestingly, George had made an earlier return visit, alone, sailing from Falmouth on Christmas Day 1915 to Lisbon. On that voyage he had given his stated country of future permanent residence as England. He will have arrived back at Santa Clara in the aftermath of Christmas. Perhaps the welcome he received changed his mind: when he sailed with Sarah in 1916 he gave his country of future residence as Spain.

A view of Santa Clara from the sea. Courtesy of Remi Fernandez Campoy

CHAPTER TEN
El Inglés de la Peseta

Sarah was not George's only companion on the return to Spain. He had acquired a spiritual companion too: Christian Science. George had converted to the religious movement, founded in the USA in the 1870s by Mary Baker Eddy. The nineteenth century had seen the rise of forms of faith and worship which deviated considerably from standard Christian worship of the time. The horror of the First World War gave a boost to some of these alternative beliefs, as orthodox Christianity had been invoked to support the war as it often had in previous European wars. One example of the popularity of alternative forms of faith was spiritualism which had grown throughout the second half of the nineteenth century but provided hope for some of those trying to cope with the loss of sons and husbands on the battlefield as Spiritualists believed it was possible to communicate with the spirits of the dead.

Mary Baker Eddy described Christian Science as a return to 'primitive Christianity and its lost element of healing'. Followers have a metaphysical belief that reality is purely spiritual and the material world an illusion: material phenomena are the result of mental states, a view expressed as 'life is consciousness' and 'God is mind.' This includes the view that disease is a mental error rather than physical disorder, and that the sick should be treated not by medicine, but by a form of prayer that seeks to correct

WHAT OUR LEADER SAYS

ELOVED CHRISTIAN SCIEN-TISTS, keep your minds so filled with Truth and Love, that sin, disease, and death cannot enter them. It is plain that nothing can be added to the mind already full. There is no door through which evil can enter, and no space for evil to fill in a mind filled with goodness. Good thoughts are an impervious armor; clad therewith you are completely shielded from the attacks of error of every sort. And not only yourselves are safe, but all whom your thoughts rest upon are thereby benefited.

The self-seeking pride of the evil thinker injures him when he would harm others. Goodness involuntarily resists evil. The evil thinker is the proud talker and doer. The right thinker abides under the shadow of the Almighty. His thoughts can only reflect peace, good will towards men, health, and holiness.

MARY BAKER EDDY

Copyright, 1909, by Mary Baker Eddy

LO QUE DICE NUESTRA CONDUCTORA

UERIDOS CIENTIFICOS CRIS-TIANOS: Tened la mente siempre tan llena de Verdad y de Amor, que ni el pecado, ni la enfermedad, ni la muerte puedan entrar en ella. Es claro que no se puede añadir nada a la mente ya llena. No hay puerta por la cual pueda entrar el mal, ni espacio que el mal pueda ocupar en una mente llena de bondad. Los buenos pensamientos son una armadura impenetrable; revestidos de ella, estaréis completamente escudados contra los ataques de toda clase de error. Y no sólo estaréis en salvo vosotros mismos, sino que también se beneficiarán todos aquellos en quienes pensáis.

El orgullo egoísta del que tiene pensamientos malos le perjudica a él mismo, cuando quiere hacer daño a los demás. La bondad resiste al mal involuntariamente. El que tiene pensamientos malos se ufana de lo que dice y hace. El que tiene pensamientos buenos mora bajo la sombra del Omnipotente. Sus pensamientos no pueden reflejar sino paz, buena voluntad hacia los hombres, salud y santidad.

MARY BAKER EDDY

Copyright, 1933, by The Trustees u/w of Mary Baker Eddy

Eddy's statement from a text owned by George. Courtesy of Remi Fernandez Campoy

the beliefs responsible for the illusion of ill health. Modern medical practice was in its infancy, and patients regularly fared better without it. This provided fertile soil for the groups such as Christian 'mind-cure' groups, who argued that sickness was an absence of 'right thinking' or failure to connect to Divine Mind.

The church does not require that Christian Scientists avoid all medical care but maintains that Christian Science prayer is most effective when not combined with medicine. The founder was strongly influenced by her Congregationalist upbringing. According to the church's tenets, adherents accept 'the inspired Word of the Bible as [their] sufficient guide to eternal Life . . . acknowledge and adore one supreme and infinite God . . . [and] acknowledge His Son, one Christ; the Holy Ghost or divine Comforter; and man in God's image and likeness.' She wrote that she wanted to 'reinstate primitive Christianity and its lost element of healing'. Evidence that George maintained this belief is found in the Appendix containing the reminiscences of Mercedes Beautell where, for example, he seeks no medical treatment for the ligament damage he has suffered playing tennis, but instead gives up tennis.

Eddy saw Jesus as a Christian Scientist, a 'Way-shower' between humanity and God, and she distinguished between Jesus the man and the concept of Christ, the latter a synonym for Truth and Jesus the first person fully to manifest it. The crucifixion was not a divine sacrifice for the sins of humanity, the atonement (the forgiveness of sin through Jesus's suffering) 'not the bribing of God by offerings', but an 'at-one-ment' with God.

After early struggles and conflicts, it became the fastest growing religion in the United States in the early twentieth century and was beginning to spread elsewhere. By 1910 there were fifty-eight churches in England. Mark Twain, writing in 1907 had described the appeal of the new religion:

> She has delivered to them a religion which has revolutionized their lives, banished the glooms that shadowed them, and filled them

and flooded them with sunshine and gladness and peace; a religion which has no hell; a religion whose heaven is not put off to another time, with a break and a gulf between, but begins here and now, and melts into eternity as fancies of the waking day melt into the dreams of sleep.

They believe it is a Christianity that is in the New Testament; that it has always been there, that in the drift of ages it was lost through disuse and neglect, and that this benefactor has found it and given it back to men, turning the night of life into day, its terrors into myths, its lamentations into songs of emancipation and rejoicing.

Once George was back at Santa Clara, he had Sebastián and Carmen, his first two employees, move his belongings from the main house to a small dwelling on the edge of the grounds close to the wall facing south west overlooking La Carihuela beach. He gave his new home the same name as the other viewpoints: El Mirador ('The Lookout'). From it he had incomparable views over the sea, the beaches and the evening sun.

Inspired by his religious faith, he began to offer a peseta to local families when they had nothing to eat. An English writer, Claire Lorrimer, who is quoted at further length below, visited Santa Clara in the 1930s as a child and observed that:

> The poverty for most of the Andalucian people was rife although we children were unaware of it. Whilst crops were harvested and sold in spring and summer, the farmers and their families were often starving in the winter when they had little or nothing to sell. The fishermen too were totally dependent on their catch.[1]

---

1   Claire Lorrimer is the pen-name of Patricia Robins (1921–2016). She published eighty novels and over a hundred books in total. Her autobiography was published under her pen-name with the title *You Never Know* (Hodder and Stoughton, 2014). Her stays in Spain inspired *Frost in the Sun,* a romantic novel set in the Spanish Civil War. The holidays in Santa Clara provided the setting for her mother's novel *Shatter the Sky,* originally published in 1933. Coronet Books, an imprint of Hodder and Stoughton, published a paperback version in 1961.

In return for their peseta, the local people from La Carihuela were required to listen to, or read if they were able, a short piece from his Christian Science tracts which were called 'tratamientos' (treatments).[1] An example of a Tratamiento, from George's belongings, courtesy of Remi Fernandez Campoy:

```
Yo soy es mi Dios, y mi Dios es Yo soy,
El bien es mi Dios, y mi Dios es el bien,
Yo soy lo que soy por el Espiritu Santo,
Yo soy perfectamente bien - y lo se,
Es la Verdad que me hace libre,
Y gracias a Dios por lo que he recibido.
```

The 'Tratamiento' translates as:

> I am is my God and my God is I am,
> The good is my God and my God is the good,
> I am what I am through the Holy Spirit,
> I am perfectly good – and I know it,
> It is truth that makes me free,
> And thanks to God for what I have received.

Christian Science urges its members to spread the word to others. It endorsed its members accepting money for teaching about its doctrine. Instead, George was giving away money to

---

1   A detailed explanation of the purpose and value of 'treatments' within Christian Science teaching can be found at http://johndoorlytrust.org/index_htm_files/FundamentalsofaCStreatmentMK_Final_V11_27112016.pdf
    An extensive biography of Mary Baker Eddy exists: G. Gill, *Mary Baker Eddy*, (Perseus Books, 1998).

George moved to a simple room in the top right sector of the photo.
Courtesy of Remi Fernandez Campoy.

The dedication to George. Courtesy of Remi Fernandez Campoy.

A silver peseta.

those who would listen to the Church's teachings. Soon he was offering the same charity to local people from the other close-by settlements of Bajondillo and Calvario and anyone else who beat a path to his door in need of help. Don Jorge soon became known as El Inglés de la Peseta. A peseta may not sound much – at the time it was worth 10*d* (ten old English pence) or 4*p* (four new English pence) – but it is said it was a day's earnings for a crewman on a fishing boat on La Carihuela. In comparison, Miriam Coles Harris says a 'Guardia Civil' was paid three pesetas a day which would equate to 60*p* for a five-day week and at the time an average weekly wage in England was £2. Before long an occasional approach to George became a routine response for many. His staff feared that he was being taken advantage of, but his charity then spread to the elderly, infirm and the poor in general and he also ended up offering lodgings to men falling on hardship after returning from the First World War.

Not surprisingly news of his actions spread and in 1918 the Town Council of Torremolinos declared him Hijo Adoptivo y Preferido (Adoptive and Favoured Son). The dedication read (translation by the author):

> It is agreed by unanimous decision to nominate don Jorge Langworthy, cavalry major of the English Army, who from the estate he owns in our municipality, by the name of Santa Clara, carries out innumerable acts of charity on a daily basis, using great sums to sustain needy families and in other philanthropic and altruistic acts, which have justly earned him the popular name of Father of the Poor . . .

No-one had hitherto been granted this title.

By now, George was employing nine staff, seven of whom lived on the estate. Over time, Sebastián and Carmen had three children. Antonio Campoy (the boatman, later George's administrator) and his wife Manuela had brought a niece to live with them and then had a daughter of their own. Three other staff lived in and the two original gardeners continued to be employed. His staff regularly prayed with George though it is not known if any of them actually converted to Christian Science. It is most likely that they did not, at least publicly. Inevitably, George's fame for charitable works underpinned by his alien faith was not well received by the Roman Catholic Church, its priests and many of its more devout worshippers.

The Town Council's recognition of George was an act of bravery or defiance. The Roman Catholic Church had dominated religious and, to a great extent, political life in Spain for well over four hundred years. Ferdinand and Isabel had set up the Inquisition in Spain in 1478, eight years after their marriage and fourteen years before they celebrated the complete Christian reconquest of Spain from Moorish rule. The interests of Church and monarchy remained strongly intertwined right up until the late twentieth century. The Protestant Reformation which began in Northern Europe in 1517 was firmly and stoutly resisted as were the ideas of the Enlightenment two hundred years later. The Inquisition was remorseless in its defence of the Roman Catholic faith against all challenges, and was not definitively abolished until 1834.[1]

In such a historical context it is not surprising that the other

1   Although in the modern era the Inquisition is indelibly linked to Spain, it was originally created in France by Pope Lucus III to counter the Albigensian heresy. It was imposed on, rather than welcomed by, some kingdoms of Spain, but in 1478, Ferdinand and Isabel requested a Papal Bull to establish an Inquisition. The motivations for, purpose, and actions of the Spanish Inqusition are still a source of historical debate, but one result was that Spain acquired a 'leyenda negra' (black legend – the opposite of a golden legend) as the epitome of a cruel, bigoted, exploitative and self-righteous nation and empire. The legend was widely propagated across Europe.

A relaxed George. Courtesy of Remi Fernandez Campoy

wealthy inhabitants of the area, urged on by the local clergy, did
everything they could to stop people going to Santa Clara and
being influenced by George, this English Protestant. A certain
don Juan Herédia and his wife, doña Luisa Huelín went so far as
to sell their estate called El Vigía, situated directly in front of the
entrance to Santa Clara, to an order of nuns called the Sisters of
Charity to become a religious college called the College of the
Miraculous Medal. They sold it for 10,000 pesetas, well below its
market value on condition that the college would deliver classes
promoting Catholicism.

At some point in the 1920s, George's wealth had all been given
away through his charitable work. It seems that some of his relatives
made a group visit in the second half of the decade. These were
perhaps nephews and nieces, though some of his brothers and sisters
were still alive. No record exists of the purpose of the visit. It may
have been triggered by the loss of his wealth, perhaps concern for
him or perhaps concern for their own prospects of an inheritance

George with his sister Ida, her husband and child. Courtesy of Remi Fernandez Campoy.

from his property. What we do know is that he died intestate and there followed a legal battle which will be explored later.

More pressingly, George was no longer able to maintain his home and staff. At this point George again might have considered, might even have been advised, to give up the property; sell it and find a small place somewhere nearby with the same views, the sea nearby, a small garden he could tend . . . He might have got a good price: the Wall Street crash of 1929 had not yet happened. Perhaps it was loyalty to his staff, but he chose to take in paying guests instead, to run a pension/hotel. He may have begun by asking his existing staff to attempt to run the operation, but in 1927, two English people, a married woman by the name of Margaret Beautell and a Mr Tick came to discuss a proposition.

'Tick' may well have been a nickname; nothing is known about him. Margaret Beautell, however is well remembered by descendants living in England and the Canary Islands. Born Margaret Horn, she had been living in Liverpool in her family home when, in about 1904, she met and fell in love with a handsome seventeen-year-old Spaniard from the Canary Islands called Manuel Beautell Meléndez. He had been sent to the city to learn about commerce. Liverpool, as a major import/export city, had long and strong commercial links with Spain. Soon Margaret was pregnant with his child but he abandoned her and returned to Tenerife. Once the baby was old enough to travel, Margaret followed Manuel to Tenerife where she told his father what had happened. The father, a respected business man on the island, persuaded Manuel to marry the mother of his child and they set up home in Santa Cruz de Tenerife where they had three more children. By 1919 Margaret had had enough of her husband's infidelities and returned with the four children to England where her father-in-law continued to support her, enabling her to send all the children to boarding school while she set up home in Llangollen, North Wales. Margaret kept up other contacts from her old life in the Canaries and in about 1926 she decided to move to Madrid where her good friend Selina Hamilton, also English, now lived. She took with her the three older children, Edith Frances (known as Nancy), Eduardo (known as Teddy) and Mercedes (known as Ita). The youngest, Alberto (Tito) stayed at school in London.

Margaret did not take to Madrid and within months had decided to try her luck in a more conducive climate and chose Málaga, leaving Eduardo to live with Selina as he had found work with General Motors. Meanwhile, her estranged husband Manuel had heard of her return to Spanish territory and stopped the maintenance allowance he had been paying her because he had never wanted her to set foot on Spanish soil again. She was, for a while, living on credit with her landlady and a local shopkeeper but a conversation with another English guest (Tick) at the pensión where she lived led to a business proposition: he had money and she wanted to establish something like a hotel or pensión as a means of earning a living for herself and her

The entrance to the hotel. Courtesy of Remi Fernandez Campoy.

daughters. Soon they heard through the expatriate English community in the city about Santa Clara and George's financial difficulties. George agreed that they could rent the *cuartel* (barracks) and run it as a hotel. Mr Tick, Margaret's new-found business partner promptly set off for England to buy what was necessary to start the business: crockery, cutlery, glassware, tea services, and a car. He also placed an advert in *The Times*: 'English family receives guests in Torremolinos.' The venture was named 'Pensión Castillo del Inglés' ('Castle of the Englishman').

The hotel-pensión had twenty-seven rooms over two floors of what was originally the barracks, surrounding a central patio. From the patio a slope rose to a great semicircular terrace which was at the front of the building and offered views over the sea, and on clear days, it was possible to see the Sierra Nevada to the east and the coast of Africa to the south. This area was known simply as *La Terraza* and Margaret became famous for serving her guests afternoon tea there. Nancy had taken charge of the hotel's linen and Mercedes, although only about sixteen, became the hotel chauffeur, often driving to Gibraltar and back to collect guests as this was the preferred route of the visiting English. The grounds and the rest of the buildings would continue as before and George stayed in El Mirador. He continued to offer what charity he could in exchange for prayer and he maintained the habit he had developed long before of visiting Annie's grave in the English Cemetery in Málaga at least once a week.

Business was going well when one day in 1929 four young graduates from the USA arrived at Santa Clara. Nancy Beautell and one of the young Americans, Mark Hawker, soon struck up a relationship, but he then moved on with his friends on their planned trip around Europe. However when the others decided to return to America, he chose to go back to Santa Clara. He had been in an orphanage in the USA as both his parents had died when he was young and he had no brothers or sisters, so little reason to return. His relationship with Nancy blossomed and in 1931 they married with the blessing not only of Margaret, but of the Beautell family in Tenerife as well.

Mark had graduated in architecture and he soon set to work improving both the gardens and the buildings and oversaw the construction of a flight of steps directly down to the beach. He also worked on raising the level of comfort to be experienced by guests.

Meanwhile, in 1930, George rented the estate to his principal male staff, namely Antonio Campoy, Pedro Gómez, Sebastián Salas and José Molina plus María Campoy, Antonio's niece. The relevant document, and a second one drawn up in 1935 were superceded by a final document in 1943 legalised in the presence of the British Consul. No actual rent was payable by them for the tenancy. The tenants were required to maintain the estates, and conserve it in the way it had been let to them and pay for repairs and outgoings plus taxes. They were entitled to receive any income from the produce of the estate including the rent due from Margaret and her family for the pensión and were authorised to offer sub-tenancies. George continued to live in El Mirador.

The original staff had lived together so long with George

that it must have felt like a family, with a total of five children, plus the Beautell children; perhaps the family that George had never been able to have with Annie. Freed of any day to day responsibilities for the whole estate, he was able to enjoy their company, and in particular sought to help with the children's development and education. He paid for Antonio's niece María to undertake a secretarial course when she was the right age. Mercedes Beautell recalls her tennis lessons with him in the brief memoir which is included as one of the appendices.

The 'family' of staff had been cultivating the grounds to grow fruit and vegetables since the time George had first acquired the estate and these could now be offered in the hotel as well as being used for their own consumption. In addition, chickens and pigs were kept on the lowest terraces. Any surplus of fruit and vegetables, along with the flowers that were so abundant in the gardens were sold locally or in Málaga.

A ready source of guests were the British, old friends and acquaintances of the Langworthys or fellow retired army officers, perhaps hearing about the place by word of mouth, but some seeing that advertisement Tick had placed in *The Times*. Britons staying in Gibraltar would make weekend outings to the hotel.

The earliest known published reference to Santa Clara in Spanish came in an article by Luis Bello. He was a writer and journalist and campaigner for good education. He toured Spain writing about all kinds of schools and one of his articles in *El Sol* newspaper praised 'La Casa del Inglés' and his school of 'simplicity and good taste'. There is no other reference to a school operating at Santa Clara, though of course, George took a delight in teaching the children of his staff anything from tennis to the English language. It may be that Bello's report indulged in a little poetic licence, but it may also have been instrumental in bringing Santa Clara to the attention of a rising group of young Spaniards, artists and intellectuals who came to be known in Spain as 'the Generation of '27'. The name arose from the fact

The Beautells and friends; (*third from left*) Margaret Horn; (*fourth from left*) Edith (Nancy); (*third from right*) Alberto (Tito); (*second from right*) Mercedes (Ita); (*right*) Eduardo (Ted). Courtesy of Carlos Beautell.

Nancy Beautell and Mark Hawker. Courtesy of Carlos Beautell

Pedlar and donkey at the entrance. Courtesy of Carlos Beautell

Path up to the entrance. Courtesy of Carlos Beautell

A bedroom in the hotel.
Courtesy of Carlos Beautell.

A sitting room in the hotel.
Courtesy of Carlos Beautell.

The most seaward of the miradores. Courtesy of Carlos Beautell

The hotel veranda. Courtesy of Carlos Beautell

Santa Clara from the air. Courtesy of Carlos Beautell

Diving off the headland. Courtesy of Carlos Beautell

Swimming off the headland. Courtesy of Carlos Beautell

The *Graf Zeppelin* over Santa Clara, 1931. Courtesy of Carlos Beautell

A group of Oxford students wait for the bus to Algeciras. Courtesy of Carlos Beautell

Santa Clara from the sea. Courtesy of Carlos Beautell

Aerial photo of the hotel and grounds. Courtesy of Francis Ternero

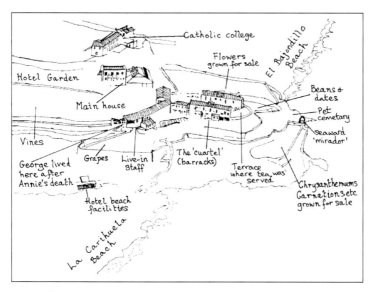

Sketch of Santa Clara as a hotel showing some of the planting recalled by Remi.
Based on photo courtesy of Francis Ternero. © Gill Shapton

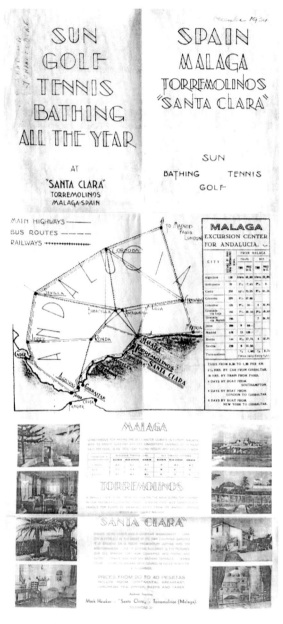

Promotional leaflet. Courtesy of Remi Fernandez Campoy

that 1927 was the tercentenary of the death of Luis de Góngora, one of Spain's great poets from their Golden Age, roughly contemporaneous with England's Elizabethan Age (Shakespeare had died in 1616).

The 'Generation of '27' was not a homogeneous group nor was it flourishing in a single location. Some of its members got to know each other in 'La Residencia de Estudiantes' in Madrid which aimed to promote progressive intellectual thought. One or more of them may have read Bello's article as *El Sol* was a Madrid daily. In Málaga a literary magazine called *Litoral* had been founded by Manuel Altolaguirre and Emilo Prados. The magazine's main source of funding was another Málaga poet, José María Hinojosa, who had private means. It was at first dedicated solely to poetry and included contributions from Federico García Lorca and other young poets experimenting with different styles of poetry, some modern, some drawing on traditional forms and sources. These poets were part of a wider artistic wakening in Spain and painters including Salvador Dalí were known to stay at the hotel. The Irish writer Ian Gibson describes Dali's time in Torremolinos in some detail.[1] Hinojosa met Dalí and his companion Gala Eluard in Paris in 1930 when Gala was recovering from a bout of pleurisy. She was also fleeing from her then husband the French poet Paul Eluard. Dalí had met Gala in 1929 in Paris where she then lived with Eluard, but they fell in love and Gala left Eluard for Dalí. Hinojosa invited the couple to spend a few weeks in Málaga to aid her convalescence. Stopping first at Barcelona they travelled from there to Málaga by train, a journey which in those days took three days.

The couple moved into the 'Castillo del Inglés'. One can

---

1   I. Gibson, *The Shameful Life of Salvador Dalí* (Faber & Faber, 1997). Gibson details Dalí's time in Santa Clara though Dalí slightly fictionalised the setting, just as Santa Clara inspired Cernuda to write his story 'El Indolente'. The painting on which Dalí worked at Santa Clara, *El Hombre Invisible* (*The Invisible Man*), is in the Museo Nacional Centro de Arte Reina Sofia in Madrid. Images of it are readily available online.

Photo of Salvador Dalí and Gala.
Copied from Gibson. Original in collection of Juan Luis Buñuel, Paris.

imagine the benefits to a convalescent in need of rest of staying in
such a quiet, beautiful out of the way place. However, Gala was
not a shy, retiring woman and Dalí recalled later that 'Gala, with
a build like a boy's, burned by the sun, would walk about the
village with her breasts bare'. Gibson reports that the locals took
this in their stride (though this seems unlikely) but it is equally
probable that Dalí is exaggerating. However, a photograph of
Gala sunbathing topless at Santa Clara is held in the archives of
the *Diario del Sur* newspaper in Málaga. Gibson reports that she
had a more dramatic effect on some of the other young poets who
encountered her. One said that 'Gala's stare struck me forcibly.
Her eyes blazed intensely as if they wished to scorch whatever
they looked at. For clothes she wore only a small red skirt and
her naked breasts, very brown and pointed were exposed with
complete naturalness to the sun.' Gala also had no inhibitions
about kissing Dalí in public, something unheard of in Spain

at the time. Dalí may well have struggled with this as he was inherently timid and shy though they were also known to parade themselves in quite garish clothes. Altolaguirre, who worked in a tourist office in Málaga, told people they were visiting Egyptians. The couple stayed five weeks at the hotel, Dalí spending most of his time working on the painting *The Invisible Man*. Their stay will hardly have enamoured George and his hotel to the local Catholic clergy and their more loyal supporters.

No record of George's view of the behaviour of Dalí and Gala, nor of the other artists' behaviour, exists. For these artists the hotel will have provided a haven from the repressive, socially conservative society that was Spain at that time. Many had spent time in France, especially Paris, a place of great artistic and social freedom. In their different ways most of them were challenging traditional artistic, social and moral values. Some, like Lorca and Luis Cernuda, were gay, Cernuda openly so. Others, like Dalí were not married to their heterosexual partners at the time. The hotel almost seems to have been a miniature foreign country straddling the promontory which had first led to the construction of the 'castillo'. They must have felt a degree of confidence to be themselves in that small enclave. It may well be that George was quite relaxed or at least did not intervene in his guests' chosen behaviours. Cernuda even incorporated George into a short story he wrote at the time, 'El Indolente', extracts from which are included in an appendix. He simply calls the character 'Don Míster' and the place 'Sansueña', but it is acknowledged to be Santa Clara.

In contrast to the libidinous behaviour of the young Spanish literati we have a child's account of staying at the hotel. Denise Robins, sometimes called 'the queen of romantic fiction', was one British artist who holidayed at Santa Clara with her children. Patricia Robins, Denise's daughter, also later a romantic novelist who used the pen-name Claire Lorrimer, wrote in her autobiography:

A couple enjoy the solitude of a mirador. Courtesy of Remi Fernandez Campoy.

My mother had found a beautiful hacienda called Santa Clara on a rocky promontory below which was a tiny sardine fishing village. The hacienda was owned by a Spanish girl who had married a Rhodes scholar and between them they had converted the stables surrounding the outer courtyard into accommodation for visitors. [*Presumably the couple were Nancy and Mark Hawker and Patricia assumed they owned it as they managed it.*] On the edge of the Mediterranean, there was a path down from the hacienda to a deserted beach. To the north were orchards of orange and lemon trees and great expanses of olive trees. Near the garden were fields of sugar cane. The place was called Torremolinos.

It is easy to imagine a child's delight in this paradise. She goes on:

We loved the donkey rides and the picnics up in the hills almost as much as we loved playing on the sandy beach which we had all to ourselves with the exception of our audience – an ever present group of small, brown-faced, dark-eyed Spanish children who came to stare mainly at my two sisters who were a curiosity to them being

A studio portrait of Denise Robins
c.1960. Copyright © estate of Denise Robins.

Karey Lierneux at Santa Clara 1932.
Did Denise borrow her name for her
heroine? Courtesy of Carlos Beautell

very blonde and blue-eyed. We also loved watching the sardine boats coming in at the end of the day and seeing the men offload their catch of fish. The village air always smelt of fish frying in olive oil. Another pleasure was to watch the owner of a herd of goats, their bells ringing when he came to our hacienda in the morning. He milked them in the yard according to our needs.

Denise Robins herself was so taken with the place that she set her 1933 romantic novel *Shatter the Sky* primarily in the hotel: 'This is the perfect place, Ralph.' These were the first words the heroine, Karey, said about her honeymoon destination: Santa Clara, Torremolinos. Robins describes the arrival of the honeymoon couple:[1]

---

1   D. Robins, *Shatter the Sky*, originally published in 1933. Coronet Books, an imprint of Hodder and Stoughton, published a paperback version in 1961. Karey seems an unusual name for the English heroine of a 1930s novel. Curiously, the Beautell family memoir *El Hotel Santa Clara y Mistress Beautell* contains a photograph of a woman called Karey Lierneux at Santa Clara in 1932.

Soon after midday they came to Torremolinos; a village of white villas and cottages and amazing flowers . . . Santa Clara . . . low built, square, with a wide veranda running right round it, and a garden which looked to Karey like Paradise itself. As they drove through the gates they passed great clumps of scarlet geranium, bold, vivid red against the white walls. Two huge palm trees stood sentinel at the gates and to the left lay the Moorish garrison which date back to 1600 and was built upon sheer rock above the sea.

Terrace after white terrace, winding down to the water. Wild pink geraniums tumbling in cascades out of the walls. Green fringe of palms; blue shimmer of anchusas in the green grass between the terraces; and the little covered huts...from which one could look straight down into the sunlit sea.

To the right lay the brown beach and a fishing village straggling along it. To the left in a haze of sunshine, Málaga, and beyond, a violet line of mountains and one snow-covered peak of Sierra Nevada . . .

Later they found themselves in the small flat which they had booked for a month. This was built in that part of the garrison called the Cuartel. A little square of low white buildings with balconies. Lemon-trees so close that one could lean out over the balcony, put out a hand and pull off a ripe fruit. At the top of the Cuartel a wide terrace; below, the sea, and everywhere the drenching sunshine.

The window of Karey's little sitting-room looked out on this terrace and down at the blue water. From the bedroom she could see the fishermen's huts on the brown beach. An oasis from the cares and worries of the world . . .

As it happens Karey had married the man who had helped her through the difficult months since the death of her adored fiancé. Her new husband had brought her here on honeymoon, but now Spain was bringing the worst out in him. Fortunately down the road, quite by chance, she discovered the cousin of her dead fiancé and he was even more attractive and in tune with her than the dead man. And so . . . but don't let me spoil it for you.

Views of La Carihuela beach. Courtesy of Remi Fernandez Campoy

To suggest that there was an eligible English bachelor down the road was not quite as far-fetched as it might sound. Gamel Woolsey, an American writer now married to Gerald Brenan living halfway between Torremolinos and Málaga wrote in 1936 that Torremolinos contained 'a large English colony eked out with foreigners of other nationalities.'

Gerald Brenan (1894–1987) was a British writer who moved to Spain after military service in the First World War. From 1920 onwards he rented a house in a village in the Alpujarras, the mountainous area facing south from the peaks of the Sierra Nevada towards the Mediterranean. In 1930, while in Dorset, he met Gamel Woolsey (1895–1968) and they married soon after. They returned to Spain and in 1934 they rented a house in Churriana, between Málaga and Torremolinos. In Spain, Brenan was highly regarded for his writing about, and enthusiasm for, the country and his house in Churriana, now an outlying suburb of Málaga, became a museum in 2014.

Another British expatriate was Sir Peter Chalmers-Mitchell.[1] (1864–1945), a zoologist, who was Secretary of the Zoological Society of London from 1903 to 1935. He created the world's first open zoological park at Whipsnade in Bedfordshire, where animals occupy large enclosures rather than cages. He first went

1   Woolsey, Brenan and Chalmers-Mitchell are referenced in the general bibliography.

to Málaga late in 1927 to visit a friend and eventually decided to retire there in 1935, anticipating a relaxed and peaceful retirement in a climate very much to his liking. The house in question was the Villa Santa Lucia 'a few minutes' walk uphill from the tramway-line and the Caleta Palace Hotel, with a lovely view of the sea and a terraced garden with sun and shade for every hour of the day'. On the other side of a neighbouring watercourse lay the estate and mansion of the rich Bolín family. His dealings with them and their mansion were to have a great influence on his time in Spain.

For both Spaniards and George and the other ex-patriates this idyll was to come to an abrupt end.

CHAPTER ELEVEN
War and a Kind of Peace

On 17 and 18 July 1936 several military garrisons rose up against the elected government of Spain. The unresolved struggle between progress and tradition that had continued for two centuries had grown ever more polarised. The three internal wars in the nineteenth century (the Carlist Wars) had deepened the rift between liberal and reactionary Spain and progressive governments, when they occurred, were repeatedly unable to achieve a consensus for change. While those areas with some industry such as Barcelona and Málaga sought investment and development, the forces of conservatism resisted. Although Spain was officially neutral in the First World War, the textile and mining industries were busy supplying both sides, with the owners making huge profits. Meanwhile there were rural food shortages and uncontrolled inflation in the towns and cities. After the First World War, there was an upsurge in industrial unrest which combined with deep political divisions and a disastrous military intervention in Morocco. Spain had lost its last colonies of Cuba, Puerto Rico and the Philippines in 1898. It was granted a residual colonial role over the northern coast of Morocco in the 1906 Algeciras agreement when the great powers carved up the Moroccan sultanate, but this was explicitly designed by Britain to frustrate France's aspiration to colonise the whole of Morocco and challenge Britain's command of the

Mediterranean sea routes through the Gibraltar Strait. However Spain's control over this territory was weak and when it tried to re-assert control in the face of attacks from Berber tribesmen in the 1920s a total of approximately 43,500 troops were killed, missing, or wounded at a financial cost which further crippled the economy.

The liberal-conservative government collapsed in 1923 when General Primo de Rivera mounted a *coup d'etat* and established a dictatorship. His economic policies looked successful for a while but the world trade crisis at the end of the decade exposed the continuing weakness of the economy. In 1930 his regime fell and soon after the monarchy was swept away amid allegations of corruption. In April 1931 a progressive alliance of republicans and socialists established the second republic. Earlier attempts at bringing about change in the country had been so often frustrated that the new government was under intense pressure to deliver on its promise of social reform. There were sporadic outbreaks of anti-establishment violence, including the burning of churches which inevitably antagonised the Catholic Church and its strongest supporters. However the new government had no dominant strategy and conflicts and tensions affected most efforts at bringing about the kinds of change those who had voted for them wanted. On top of the political stalemate, the effects of the 1929 financial crash were felt most strongly in Spain in 1933. Social tensions increased; the social divisions were huge; politics was polarised. In 1931 almost the whole of Spain's southern and eastern seaboard (and inland for about one hundred kilometres), from the Portuguese border in the south west to the French border in the northeast was predominantly Anarchist. In Spain this meant a preference for government to be local rather than central – more akin to what is known as federalism in other European countries. Central and western Spain was mainly Socialist. Northern Spain was predominantly Catholic/conservative. In the general election in February 1936 these Anarchist/Socialist areas were those that voted primarily for the elected Popular Front government which was attacked and finally defeated by the military rebels.[1] When the war started in July 1936, Málaga was in government territory though the land to the west, including that bordering Gibraltar, was in the hands of the rebels.

From the distance of over eighty years it is easy to forget that the people who governed Spain from 1939 to 1975 were the rebels in this conflict. Senior military officers, amongst them Francisco Franco, co-ordinated the rebellion. Franco quickly emerged as the leading general and went on to be dictator of Spain from his triumph in the Civil War in 1939 until his death in 1975. His internal support came from the wealthy, especially landowners, the aristocracy and the Roman Catholic Church and they advocated the restoration of the monarchy (which did not come about until Franco's death). His victory was aided by the active participation of the military forces of both Germany and Italy who were now governed by Hitler and Mussolini respectively. For clarity these forces will be referred to as the rebels or Nationalists, though their opponents usually called them Fascists.

They launched their rebellion against the democratically elected government who will be termed the Republicans, though the Nationalists preferred to call them Reds. As outlined above this Popular Front government's support came from a variety of political groupings which had barely had time to debate and attempt to iron out their differences since their success in the national elections only five months before the military rebellion. Consequently it proved difficult to achieve a unified response, especially as some groupings in the Popular Front, such as the Anarchists (strong in the Málaga region for example) were inherently against centralised control. One reaction to news of the rebellion was for some political groupings to urge revolution before the right-wing rebellion could take hold. In Málaga a

---

1 For a sample of the many books on the civil war, see the bibliography.

Committee of Public Safety controlled most of the city consisting mainly of members of CNT-FAI (National Confederation of Labour/Iberian Anarchist Federation). Known right-wingers were rounded up and imprisoned. It is estimated that more than a thousand were executed in the seven months that the city remained in Republican hands. Many of these were executed in reprisal for rebel air raids which had killed inhabitants of the city and for which crowds demanded retribution.

Young supporters of the government mobilise in 1936. See http://www.malagahistoria.com

Apart from the infighting which actually escalated between Republican factions as the war went on, the Republican government received little help on the international stage. Britain, France, Germany Italy, the USSR and other countries signed a non-intervention agreement in August 1936, but Nazi Germany and Fascist Italy ignored this and supplied men and hardware to the rebels...and the hardware was modern. The planes that bombed places like Guernica were German planes flown by German pilots. Some of the ships which bombarded the Mediterranean coast were

Italian ships crewed by Italians. In contrast, the USSR supplied arms to the Republican government in return for Spanish gold reserves, but much of what they supplied was antiquated. France and Britain, Spain's most powerful democratic neighbours, remained neutral as part of their policy of appeasement of Hitler. The only help that came from these countries was in the form of individual citizens fundraising and joining the International Brigades which fought in the Republican army.

Damage in Málaga at the start of the war. See http://www.malagahistoria.com

In the first words of her account of outbreak of the Civil War, Gamel Woolsey captured the diversity of the Republicans: 'The lorries came thicker and faster, brandishing pistols, bristling with rifles, singing the Internationale. They were chalked with the initials of all the Left parties, U.G.T. Socialists, C.N.T. Anarcho-Syndicalists, F.A.I. the extreme anarchists.'

Immediately, half the buildings on the Calle Larios, the expensive shopping street were burned along with many houses in La Caleta, a prosperous suburb.

British citizens await embarkation 25 July 1936. See http://www.malagahistoria.com

Quickly the British consul in Málaga had arranged for a destroyer to take off British citizens to Gibraltar from where they could make their way back to the UK if they wished. Word got round to assemble at Santa Clara from where anxious people could see the destroyer anchored offshore. In time they were told to go to Málaga to board it, but it would not leave till the next day when people further afield could reach the city. Woolsey and Gerald Brenan had decided not to go and Woolsey was quite scathing about the British who were leaving:

> While we sat talking . . . we looked around at the refugees. They were not the anxious, flying possessionless creatures one usually associates with that word, but well-fed, well-dressed members of the richer classes who had had good breakfasts and baths that morning and would most probably have them tomorrow morning too.

While this was happening Mark Hawker and Nancy's brother Eduardo (Teddy) were absent from Santa Clara. An American journalist by the name of Jay Allen who had abandoned his own house in Torremolinos and taken refuge at the hotel asked Mark to drive him to Gibraltar to fetch some important papers that had arrived for him from the USA. Nancy's brother Eduardo went with them. As they were entering the town of La Línea, adjacent to Gibraltar, someone opened fire on the car. Eduardo was shot in the shoulder and the car ended up with twenty-one bullet holes in a garage in La Línea after which the family never saw it again. In 1936 the whole of this part of Spain remained in the hands of forces who supported the elected government, but law and order had broken down and anywhere could be dangerous. The US consul urged Mark to send Nancy and their baby daughter out of the country and, as a British citizen, Nancy was entitled to take advantage of the British measures to remove its citizens from the country by ship. Mark insisted on staying arguing that they had put so much of their lives into Santa Clara that he was determined to fight for it. In fact, Nancy does not seem to have gone further than Gibraltar where her second child, a son, Mark (junior), was born on 17 November 1936. Mark appears to have tried to find work in Tangier and in Gibraltar as the hotel had now stopped functioning as such, but before the summer of 1937 they were all back at Santa Clara.

Málaga was in a curious position when the Civil War started. Many in Spain who were politically aware were not surprised when the uprising began. Unrest had simmered since the collapse of the dictatorship in 1930 and the emergence of progressive forces. The wealthy and the Church were not going to cede things easily to the forces of reform. Punitive repression had continued despite the wishes of the more progressive voices in government, most notably after the miners' strike in Asturias in 1934. In 1938 Sir Peter Chalmers Mitchell published the record of his experiences in his short-lived stay in Spain as *My House in Málaga*. His reading of the situation was that as soon as the left-wing won the elections in February 1936, serious preparations for an armed uprising began immediately and a 'number of the more wealthy Spaniards at once began to leave the country, taking with them, or exporting against the law, their money and their portable valuables'. In Málaga there was an attempt at an uprising as part of the scheduled events of mid-July. A young lieutenant in the regular army led his forces to the Civil Governor but the Assault Guards remained loyal and the lieutenant's men were captured

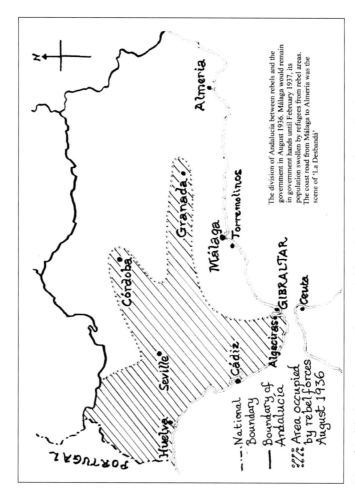

Map of Andalucía in August 1936 showing rebels' rapid advance north and west of Málaga. © Gill Shapton from R. Fraser, *Blood of Spain*.

The division of Andalucía between rebels and the government in August 1936. Málaga would remain in government hands until February 1937, its population swollen by refugees from rebel areas. The coast road from Málaga to Almería was the scene of 'La Desbandá'

or surrendered. News of the uprising triggered an initial wave of lawlessness among sections of the dominant left-wing. These will have been responsible for the shooting up of Mark Hawker's car at La Línea and will have explained the lorries witnessed by Woolsey travelling to and fro in the first days.

However, the city was not occupied by rebel forces until February 1937. Within a month of hostilities starting in July 1936 the rebels held most of the other Andalucian cities: Cadiz, Sevilla, Córdoba, Granada. But the coastal area from Gibraltar eastward remained in the hands of people loyal to the government.

Although people seen as supporting the rebellion were rounded up and imprisoned, and as described above, possibly one thousand were executed, Chalmers-Mitchell is adamant that the brutality and savagery reported by the rebels and repeated by ex-patriates leaving the country did not take place. Woolsey published her account of the start of the civil war in 1939 in *Death's Other Kingdom*. The burning of the city she describes happened in those first days when the Republicans, furious that conservative forces were rebelling against their progressive government, turned on the properties of the rich and burned their houses and shops in the centre of the city. Wolsey and Brenan could see this from their house. The next day they walked the few miles to Torremolinos to visit an American journalist friend (not the same one as Hawker drove to Gibraltar) 'as we felt he ought to understand better than the rest of us what was really happening'. Soon after, once the roads were re-opened they made a trip into Málaga to see the damage for themselves. Clearly some people had reacted violently to the news of the insurgency as she describes above, but she noticed that 'Groups of calm, intelligent-looking young workmen were going about quietly repairing the damage as far as they were able . . .'

From the accounts of both Woolsey and Chalmers Mitchell, many expatriates were sympathetic to the rebels and had been apprehensive about the new left-wing government. In terms of

Villa Santa Lucía, Málaga. From P. Chalmers-Mitchell, *My House in Málaga*.

Sir Peter Chalmers-Mitchell. From P. Chalmers-Mitchell, *My House in Málaga*.

the Spanish social order of the time they were privileged, they lived in the better neighbourhoods or on land adjacent to wealthy Spaniards in the surrounding countryside, so these were the Spaniards with whom they socialised, when they were not in the English Club in Málaga. This applied too to Woolsey, Brenan and Chalmers Mitchell. While all three were sympathetic to the democratically elected Republican government, but on a personal level they were only too keen to help those that they knew, who also tended to be wealthier Spaniards, so in due course, this made their situation difficult. Woolsey and Brenan supported, and then hid, an impoverished aristocratic family who nevertheless earned increasing disfavour especially as the head of the family would publicly celebrate rebel achievements such as the bombing of the heavy oil terminal in Málaga docks. Eventually they helped them leave the country but Woolsey says, 'Our position was never very pleasant again . . . They [the general citizens and the civil authorities] were not so sure of the innocence and simplicity of the English as they had been.' She became more nervous for their safety as bombs from air raids dropped close to their house. 'Our leaving of Spain in the end was a kind of accident. We decided to go to Gibraltar to get some money . . . the boat which was leaving was an American destroyer . . . Málaga . . . grew small and smaller until the destroyer, gathering speed, drew rapidly out to sea . . .'

Chalmers Mitchell stayed much longer but one of his major difficulties was helping out his neighbours, who happened to be a wealthy family of aristocrats called Bolín. The head of the family, don Tomás was taken into custody as a supporter of the rebels, but Chalmers Mitchell took in the family, don Tomás's mother, wife and five daughters, when they abandoned their mansion. He also himself searched the house for anything which may have further incriminated the family in the eyes of the civil authorities. He says he acted in good faith, believing the family when they claimed that they were in no way associated with the Nationalists, though he later realised that this was not true, and his efforts in protecting them from harm could have jeopardised his own welfare. As more and more people were being injured by Nationalist air-raids and wounded refugees were arriving in Málaga in increasing numbers, the Bolín's mansion was converted into a hospital (with the very grudging acceptance of Señora Bolín). Chalmers Mitchell is at pains to point out how much care was taken by the 'Reds' to avoid harm coming to the family's valuables. He continued to ignore the British Consul's urgings to leave and in September even managed, with great difficulty, to get the Bolín grandmother and the five daughters out on a British ship. Later he even got the aristocrat himself and his wife onto a British warship under the noses of the authorities, and this time he left too. Back in England he wrote to *The Times* and addressed public meetings to try and change public opinion which had been heavily influenced by pro-Nationalist propaganda. In December he began his return to Spain via Gibraltar and a British destroyer. He brought as many foodstuffs and medical supplies for the hospital next door as he could carry. Everything was becoming difficult to obtain in the surrounded city.

Málaga after the entrance of troops February 1937. See http://www.malagahistoria.com

Ironically, in July 1936, the nephew of the family that Chalmers Mitchell had helped, Luis Bolín, had organised the flight of the plane from Croydon in the UK to the Canary Islands which transported General Franco from the Canaries to Morocco. Franco arrived on 19 July in Tetuán to lead the insurrection and prepare the transport of the troops to the mainland from Ceuta.

The troops that finally took the city and the surrounding area including Torremolinos in February 1937 were Italian. The people offered little resistance. Fast, light Italian tanks moved swiftly into the city. The rebel troops were under the command of General Queipo de Llano one of the most ruthless and vengeful rebel commanders. Nearly four thousand Republicans were shot. The numbers arrested led to the opening of two concentration camps, one of them in Torremolinos, on the land known as the Cortijos del Moro. Refugees, including the many who had already arrived from the direction of Ronda and Antequera flooded out of the city on the road to Almería, the only apparent way of escape. It has been estimated that there were more than 100,000 people strung out without food and water on what became known as El Camino de la Muerte (The Road of Death). They were shelled from the sea, bombed from the air and machine-gunned by the pursuing Italian units. The Nationalists' treatment of Málaga and the surrounding area counts as one of the single worst atrocities of the Civil War. Eyewitnesses included *The Times'* correspondent Lawrence Fernsworth. The event is still known as La Desbandá (the exodus). It has been suggested that if Picasso had known about it, his most famous painting *Guernica* may instead have been about Málaga. Málaga was the city of his birth though he left with his family at the age of ten and never lived there again.

Chalmers Mitchell was still in the city in January 1937 as the arrival of rebel troops became increasingly likely. 'For the next three weeks, and, until my arrest by Franco's officers on February 9, I lived a quiet and almost isolated life . . .' he tells his readers. On 21 January the British Consul had received orders from London to burn all papers he could not remove and go to Gibraltar on HMS *Antelope*, currently on guard off Málaga. Other Britons left with him. Chalmers-Mitchell stayed. On 3 February, two foreign journalists arrived at his house, Gerda Grepp, a Norwegian, and the Hungarian Arthur Koestler, then a journalist for the *News Chronicle* in London, but later best known for his novel about Soviet Russia *Darkness at Noon*. He also wrote about his experiences in the Civil War in *Spanish Testament*. Rebel radio broadcasts warned that Málaga would soon be taken. Refugees continued to pour into the city. Koestler and Grepp went out along the coast road to the east and Koestler persuaded Grepp to go on to Valencia, now the seat of the elected Republican government, while he returned to Chalmers Mitchell's house. When they were arrested on 9 February, the officer in charge was no other than the same Luis Bolín who had organised Franco's clandestine flight. Chalmers Mitchell got word to the Acting British Consul and the following morning he was released to the custody of the captain of HMS *Basilisk* which promptly sailed to Gibraltar. Chalmers-Mitchell immediately alerted the *News Chronicle* to Koestler's situation but Koestler ended up in a death cell in the prison in Seville. His life was only saved when he was exchanged for a 'high value' rebel prisoner. Chalmers Mitchell never returned to Spain. Woolsey and Brenan returned in 1953 and their remains are in the English Cemetery in Málaga, not too far from the remains of Annie and George.

It is very likely that George continued to make regular trips to Málaga, at least to visit Annie's grave. He will have been well-known and easily recognisable in the city, just like Chalmers-Mitchell. They shared, too, a belief that being British subjects rendered them immune to arrest or detention, though it is true that Chalmers-Mitchell finally concluded that he was in danger. George was an ex-soldier, and in addition to being battle-hardened albeit many years previously, the nature of his religious faith will have strengthened his resolve to carry on as near normal as possible.

At Santa Clara the British and American flags were both flown and these appear to have helped it be regarded as neutral territory, though some troops were quartered in the lower rooms of the old barracks section. This did have the advantage that those inside Santa Clara enjoyed some foodstuffs that were a scarcity amongst the local population. However it did not have the ability to protect Mark. One day in October 1937 Nationalist soldiers appeared at the hotel in search of him. He was arrested and taken away without explanation along with a British subject by the name of Herbert Merrick, a senior civil servant in Gibraltar. They were soon released, but Mark never felt safe in Spain again. The couple's third and last child, Margaret, was born at Santa Clara in August 1938, but soon after the end of the Civil War the family left for the United States and settled in California

At some point after the Nationalist takeover, two of George's staff, Sebastián Salas and Antonio Campoy, were also detained. When George heard about it, he called the staff together to spend the night praying for them using the passages they were all familiar with from his Christian Science prayer book. The next day George went to talk to the local authorities about them and was advised that they had been taken to the bullring in Málaga where everyone arrested was taken awaiting trial. He ordered that his car be readied immediately and he set off for Málaga that same morning. He was back the same day with both men safe and sound. He had succeeded in negotiating their release and possible saving their lives.

The Spanish, British and US flags fly above Santa Clara. Courtesy of Remi Fernandez Campoy.

The concentration camp in Torremolinos was one of many set up to hold captured Republicans who were later used as slave labour. The area is now bordered by the Casa de la Cultura in the El Calvario district of the town, the Aquapark and the Palma de Mallorca school. The camp was open air without barracks or latrines. By the end of the Civil War it is estimated that there were four and a half thousand prisoners in there. Knowledge of the camp may well have brought back to George unpleasant memories of how the British treated the Boers and black Africans in South Africa.

George Langworthy,
his last studio portrait.
Courtesy of Remi Fernandez
Campoy.

After the war ended on 1 April 1939, Torremolinos, like much of Spain, was devastated. The town looked nothing like the symbol of modernity it had become before the civil war. The bombs and attacks from both sides had left it in ruins. Economically, the whole country was wretched, showing the ravages of a vicious internecine conflict. The shortage of even the most basic foods affected everybody, but worst of all the poor, who had to join long queues with their ration cards. It is estimated that up to 200,000 Spaniards starved to death or died of diseases linked to malnutrition in the years 1939–45. In Santa Clara they were fortunate because they had the produce from the grounds. Thanks to those fruits and vegetables the residents did not experience the hunger that prevailed outside the walls.

Recovery from the war was slow everywhere, but the pre-war fame of Torremolinos as a holiday destination served it well, and the tourists began to return. A new couple took over running the hotel after the Hawkers had left for the USA: Frederick and Edith Saunders. In 1942 a hotel called La Roca opened very close to Santa Clara, but its opening did not undermine business at Santa Clara, rather the opposite as they embarked on new publicity, hailing Torremolinos as 'the paradise of Spain. A spring climate all the year round.'

George, meanwhile, continued with his religious devotions and his regular visits to Annie's grave in Málaga and it was on one of those visits in 1944 that he fell while getting off a tram and broke his hip. The accident confined him to bed and in keeping with his religious beliefs he would not accept medical interventions. Early in 1945 he developed a pneumonia which cost him his life. He died in Torremolinos on 29 April 1945 at six o'clock in the evening.

CHAPTER TWELVE
George's Legacy

George died without making a will. His surviving relatives, mainly his nephews and nieces sought to declare their right to inherit his estate. The staff continued to live at Santa Clara, exercising their rights as tenants under the document signed by George in 1943 and maintaining the arrangement with the Saunders to manage the hotel. The name was changed from Hotel-Pensión Castillo del Inglés to Hotel Santa Clara.

Maria Campoy with her husband Manuel and her children Miguel and Remi.
Courtesy of Remi Fernandez Campoy.

In 1951 George's relatives concluded a sale of the property for 850,000 pesetas. The staff sought to have the sale halted and also attempted to sue Saunders for sixteen months unpaid rent. They lost on both counts and what is worse, the courts declared that they did not recognise the tenancy agreement between the staff and George, that the Saunders were the direct tenants of the heirs to the estate, namely George's family, and the family had every right to follow through the sale given that the Saunders did not exercise their prior right to purchase the property. While the lawsuit progressed the hotel continued to function as normal, but George's original tenants began to despair that they would lose their home and their livelihood. Then by chance their plight came to the attention of a well-connected guest who relayed the details of the case to a lawyer with connections to a minister in Franco's government. In due course the Supreme Court found in favour of the staff and the purchase money was returned to the intended buyer.[1]

With the help of the same lawyer, the staff formed a partnership with other investors and in 1961 sold the whole estate to a wealthy Spanish businessman.Then the inevitable happened. The charms of the old hotel did not appeal any more either as a private home to a wealthy entrepreneur, nor as an attractive destination to the new tourists, nor a profitable enterprise when surrounded by the sparkling new high-rises. Demolition of the original buildings began as soon as 1962, but constructing a replacement was plagued by delays and it was not until August 1975 that the new Hotel Castillo de Santa Clara was opened. It was an 'apartotel' consisting of 140 apartments and 224 hotel rooms catering for 900 people all completed to standards that were regarded as luxurious at the time.

The tourist boom was in full swing. The summer streets were thronged with north Europeans in search of their fortnight of pleasure. Now, in the twenty-first century, even that phase has passed and although still a busy resort, home-ownership by Europeans from those same countries balances out the visiting tourist, and for Spaniards the economy and the politics are unrecognisable from the days when the tourist boom began.

---

1   A detailed account of the legal battle over ownership, and the subsequent sale and re-development can be found in one of the four Spanish language books cited previously: Comunidad de Proprietarios La Cornisa de Santa Clara Torremolinos' *El Castillo de Santa Clara. Un Lugar Emblemático* (Ediciones del Genal of Málaga, 2015)

Dedication to Margaret Beautell. © Mike Shapton

George and Annie are remembered with wall plaques on the site of their former home, the approach road is called Calle del Castillo del Inglés and in Málaga their graves in the English Cemetery have been restored to their former grace. Recently an additional dedication has been made to 'Mistress Beautell' for her role in the successful conversion of George's home into the first hotel on the Costa del Sol. Local people who are interested in the history of their town are keen to guard the memory of these English people who did so much to chart the course of the town's development.

It is possible to think of George as a man whose life was divided by the two centuries in which he lived. In the nineteenth century he was a rising cavalry officer, wealthy, accomplished, who finally fell in love and married a beautiful young woman. As soon as he steps into the twentieth century he enters the war which disillusioned so many like him, he emerged from it with a severe wound, and after believing he had found his own corner of paradise where he could lead a new life with his bride, he loses her to illness within a few short years of their time together. The following year he does his patriotic duty and returns to his homeland to help the war effort. By the time he could no longer offer his services he will have known the enormous sacrifice of human life the war was exacting. It is probably while he was in England that he discovered Christian Science and perhaps it began to help him banish the gloom and find some gladness and peace. As a military man of his time he would have had little patience with himself if he could not shake off or rise above any grief he was feeling for his wife's death, especially when he knew so many of his compatriots were losing fathers, sons and husbands to the war. Perhaps he felt that the beauty of nature in Santa Clara combined with the beauty they had created in the grounds had completed the healing of his own body and mind after the war in South Africa. Perhaps he felt that the medicine of his time had failed to save Annie. Undoubtedly he would have called on the best doctors available in Málaga or Gibraltar to treat her, but to no avail. He did not deviate from this belief in respect of himself, as recalled by Mercedes Beautell in her brief memoir contained in an appendix. While few now would subscribe to his belief, very many would testify to the restorative power of a holiday on the Spanish coast.

CHAPTER THIRTEEN
Travellers, Settlers, Artists and Tourists

The point at which George's home became the first hotel on the Costa del Sol is now recognised as a turning point in the area's development. But it was not the start of the idea that foreign travel offered opportunities for personal development or even simply for leisure. In terms of the behaviour of the British, a good starting point is the end of the Napoleonic Wars. The French Revolution and then the rise of Napoleon put paid to the practice of wealthy Britons making the Grand Tour which had started in the seventeenth century and became more popular in the eighteenth. The focus of this tour was the Greco-Roman heritage which had fuelled the Renaissance, propelling Western Europe into a new era of learning and enlightenment. France was a necessary and valued part of these journeys but the Revolution and Napoleon's rise made visiting and travelling through France impossible for the British. After his defeat people were keen to resume their travels, but those who had visited Paris before the Revolution now found it disappointingly full of . . . tourists. So what is the difference between a tourist and a traveller?

For my purpose I am going to see a traveller as someone whose destination is not well known or frequented by his compatriots; whose journey is at least a little arduous, unpredictable, perhaps even slightly dangerous and who has to exercise some degree of initiative to get there. A tourist I will define as someone for whom effectively, those characteristics do not exist: others have gone before her or him; the route and the destination are known and predictable, and perhaps even those at the receiving end know what and who to expect. A settler would be someone who stops there if not permanently then at least for a good while. Tourists tend to follow where travellers have been, at least when the traveller reports on things that are attractive to the tourist. Britons have travelled to many places where tourists would not choose to go. When the Grand Tour started it had many elements of the former: even travelling to Italy was dangerous, but by the time it was killed off by the political situation in France it could probably be described as tourism. In fact it is said that many who were ostensibly going to see the cultural icons of Western civilisation were spending most of their time in bars, brothels and casinos. Who would have thought it?

So, if France, Italy and Greece were old hat, where next? Many who had fought in Spain for or against Napoleon came back with tales of what had in many ways been a closed country. It was an unfamiliar, in some ways exotic, place. In Northern Europe the Romantic Movement was well under way. Romanticism was a reaction to scientific rationalism and the Industrial Revolution. It valued the emotional and the individual, glorifying the past and Nature. Suddenly Spain epitomised the Romantic mood. The novella *Carmen* by the Frenchman Prosper Merimée, published in 1845 captured this spirit. Merimée set the story in 1820. The first we hear about Carmen, a beautiful young tobacco factory worker, is that she has attacked a woman with a knife. She goes on to bring about the downfall of the soldier whom she says she loves and who has fallen in love with her, but she has now gone with a bullfighter. When she scorns the soldier he stabs her as the bullfighter is celebrating a victory in the ring. Thirty years later the story was turned into an opera by Georges Bizet and remains hugely popular. This is Spain: exotic, individualistic, emotional, violent. To this day many north Europeans see the Spanish temperament this way, though in truth it is more a reflection of an Andalucian image of Spain. It would be hard to envisage *Carmen* set in a rainy Asturian mining town. An American writer, Washington Irving, (author of 'Rip van Winkle') published *Tales of the Alhambra; A Series of Tales and Sketches of the Moors and Spaniards* in 1832 after being captivated by Granada and its Moorish palace. The blend of European and Arabic history called travellers to explore Spain.

Two influential books appeared in England in the space of as many years: George Borrow's *The Bible in Spain* (1843) and Richard Ford's *A Handbook for Travellers in Spain* (1845). Borrow travelled by horseback right through the heart of Spain printing and distributing copies of the New Testament on behalf of the Bible Society. His book sold well in the UK, the USA and was translated into French and German. Ford travelled extensively throughout northern Europe but spent 1830 to 1833 in Andalucía for the benefit of his wife's failing health. His book continued to be reprinted well into the twentieth century.

Another French author who travelled in Spain in 1840, Theophile Gautier, wrote a vivid account of what it meant to be a traveller there:

> Une enterprise périlleuse et romanesque . . . Les privations, l'absence des choses les plus indispensables à la vie, le danger des routes vraiment impracticables, une chaleur infernale, un soleil à fendre le crane, sont les moindres inconvénients; vous avez en outre les factieux, les voleurs, les hoteliers . . .

> A perilous and Romanesque enterprise . . . the deprivations, the absence of the things most indispensable to life, the danger of truly impractible routes, an infernal heat a sun to boil the head are the least of the inconveniences ; you also have the trouble-makers, the thieves, the hoteliers . . .

(Author's translation)

By the 1860s the difficult journeys that these early travellers and writers had faced were beginning to be eased. Steamships were replacing sailing ships especially on routes not requiring long oceanic passages, and the railway was spreading its tendrils throughout Europe. In 1865 a line reached Málaga from Córdoba. The day of the tourist loomed, but it was not a simple separation. Travellers continued to reach Spain well into the twentieth century. Here are two more English ones.

Laurie Lee (1914–1997) left his Gloucestershire village in 1934, determined to travel but with no specific destination beyond London in mind. After working on a building site in London,

> I . . . suddenly realized one morning that once the job was finished I could go anywhere I liked in the world . . . Europe at least was wide open, a place of casual frontiers, few questions and almost no travellers. So where should I go? . . . France, Italy, Spain? I knew nothing at all about any of them . . . Then I remembered that somewhere or other I picked up a phrase in Spanish for 'Will you please give me a glass of water?' and it was probably this rudimentary bit of lifeline that finally made up my mind. I decided to go to Spain.

He took a ship to Vigo and effectively walked from Spain's north-west tip to the Mediterranean coast, ending up at Almuñecar, equipped only with his violin and his easy charm to get him by.

Rose Macaulay (1881–1958) travelled alone by car from the French border at Port Bou to the Portuguese border at Ayamonte and beyond to Cape St Vincent at Portugal's south-western tip in 1949. She followed the coastline, or 'Fabled Shore', the title she gave her book. This merits the title 'travelling' rather than tourism. Most women would not have contemplated travelling alone at that point, especially in a country where very conservative attitudes to women had been re-imposed following Franco's victory in the Civil War only ten years previously. The roads in the impoverished, war-torn county will have been unpredictable and often in poor repair. Motor cars were none too reliable in that era. But travel she did, turning up in Torremolinos. She describes her approach from Málaga.

> The mountains had withdrawn a little from the sea; the road ran a mile inland; the sunset burned on my right, over the vines and canes and olive gardens. I came into Torremolinos, a pretty country place, with, close on the sea, the little Santa Clara hotel, white and tiled and rambling, with square arches and trellises and a white-walled garden dropping down by stages to the sea.

Macaulay was a keen swimmer, always taking the chance to cool off from the Spanish heat:

> One could bathe either from the beach below, or from the garden, where a steep, cobbled path twisted down the rocks to a little terrace, from which one dropped down into ten feet of green water heaving gently against a rocky wall. A round full moon rose corn-coloured behind a fringe of palms. Swimming out to sea, I saw the whole of the bay, and the Málaga lights twinkling in the middle of it . . . Behind the bay the dark mountains reared with here and there a light. It was an exquisite bathe. After it I dined on a terrace in the garden; near me three young Englishmen were enjoying themselves with two pretty Spanish girls they had picked up in Málaga; they knew no Spanish, the señoritas no English, but this made them all the merrier. They were the first English tourists I had seen since I entered Spain; they grew a little intoxicated, and they were also the first drunks I had seen in Spain. They were not very drunk, but one seldom sees Spaniards drunk at all.

Macaulay, like Robins pre-war, was captivated by the setting of Santa Clara:

> I got up early next morning and went down the garden path again to

bathe. There were blue shadows on the white garden walls and cactuses and aloes above them, and golden cucumbers and palms. I dropped into the green water and swam out; Málaga across the bay was golden pale like a pearl; the little playa of Torremolinos had fishing boats and nets on it and tiny lapping waves. Near me was a boat with fishermen, who were hacking mussels off the rocks and singing. The incredible beauty of the place and hour, of the smooth opal morning sea, shadowing to deep jade beneath the rocks, of the spread of the great bay, of the climbing, winding garden above with the blue shadows on its white walls, the golden pumpkins, the grey-green spears of the aloes, the arcaded terrace and rambling jumble of low buildings was like the returning memory of a dream long forgotten.

Denise Robins, the romantic novelist, could arguably be called an early tourist because when she went to Torremolinos with her children and their governess, certainly when she returned for repeat holidays, she knew the details and nature of the journey and her destination. Perhaps on that same journey the children could still be called travellers as young children have no clear idea of what lies in store. Here's her daughter, Patricia (the author Claire Lorrimer) on the journey:

> To get there we had a horrible four-day boat trip to Gibraltar, there being no aeroplane service in those days. Nor did the boats have stabilizers and I was invariably seasick when we sailed through the Bay of Biscay. From Gibraltar we were driven by taxi along the coast road to Málaga. The sides of the road were cobbled as the main form of transport consisted of donkeys. These were laden with heavy panniers hanging from their sides and as often as not, a man sat astride the heavily laden animal as well.

We will return to the question of tourists later, but chronologically we need to look at some settlers, those who travel and stay for whatever reason.

Málaga as noted, had a sizeable north European community settled there when George and Annie arrived. The main reason for their presence was commercial. They were there to run businesses, to trade, to make money. There are, as well, a few Britons that we know about through their writings who had made this area their home.

Gerald Brenan (1894–1987), as mentioned earlier, moved to Spain after service in the army in the First World War, settling in the Alpujarras, on the coastal side of the Sierra Nevada. In 1931 he married the American poet Gamel Woolsey and in 1935 he bought a house in Churriana on the west side of Málaga, but convenient for Torremolinos and its popular Hotel Santa Clara. It was from this house in Churriana, on the Calle Torremolinos, that they witnessed the scenes that Woolsey described in her book *Death's Other Kingdom* on the first days of the Civil War. Although they supported the Republicans, they fled Spain weeks after the war started as they had been sheltering the aristocrat Carlos Crooke Larios, a supporter of the rebels, from whom they had bought the house and who had become a friend. They felt vulnerable to attack by the other side as well as the rebels' planes had begun bombing raids on the city and their house was near the new airport. Brenan was banned from Spain by Franco until 1953 because of his outspoken criticism of the dictator. They returned and lived in the house until Woolsey's death in 1968. A host of leading figures stayed with them there including the poet E. E. Cummings, Bertrand Russell, Laurence Olivier, Vivien Leigh, Orson Welles and Ernest Hemingway. In his final years, Brenan was moved – in controversial circumstances – to a nursing home in England in 1984, but he returned to Spain after the authorities there made special arrangements to provide him with the nursing care on which he depended. His ashes are buried next to Woolsey in the English cemetery in Málaga.

Marjorie Grice-Hutchinson, MBE (1908–2003) was an English economist who obtained a Ph.D. from the London

School of Economics under the supervision of the Anglo-Austrian economist Frederick Hayek. She taught Spanish at King's College London and later lived in Spain. She is best known for her work on the School of Salamanca, a group of Spanish economists whose thinking was centuries ahead of European economics elsewhere. She married a German-born agronomist Ulrich, Baron von Schlippenbach, who already lived in Málaga where she joined him in 1951 and remained for the rest of her life. She was the recipient of many academic awards. She became a close friend of Gamel Woolsey and wrote an account of living in Málaga in the 1950s called *Málaga Farm* which was not translated into Spanish until her final years. The University of Málaga's botanical garden is on an estate originally bought by her father in 1924 and donated to the University by her.

Sir Peter Chalmers-Mitchell (1864–1945), who provided us with a vivid account of the build-up and first months of the Civil War had intended to settle in Spain. He had first come to Málaga to visit a friend who was wintering in the Caleta Palace Hotel because of her ill-health. He had helped her find a villa to rent, the Villa Santa Lucia which is where he lived when he came to retire in Spain in 1935, his friend having passed away. Apart from writing two volumes of memoir, he translated three novels by a Spanish author. He was known to the locals as 'Sopita' (pronounced 'Sorpeeta') and when Koestler came to Málaga looking for him in February 1937 he could only find his way to Sir Peter's house when a local realised he was looking for 'Sopita' which is how he is still remembered. Koestler called him the Grand Old Man of Málaga, 'sitting at his writing desk in the light of an oil lamp, apparently oblivious to what is going on outside – a perfect Victorian idyll in the midst of the apocalyptic flood'. Koestler dedicated his book *Spanish Testament* about the Civil War to Sir Peter.

The Spanish Civil War and the Second World War between them drove away many of the settlers (though George never left Santa Clara) and killed off the fledgling tourist industry of prosperous adventurous Britons and others. Spain was more impoverished than ever, Europe drained by six years of war, though the USA enjoyed an economic boom and many of its citizens had discovered Europe in military uniform. In the postwar world order, Franco, although helped greatly by Hitler and Mussolini in his victory over the then elected government, was now accepted as an ally because of the new politics of the Cold War. The USA opened two military bases in southern Spain, Rota naval base at Cadiz in 1955 and Morón airbase near Seville in 1956. The presence of service personnel from these bases was mentioned in a novel, *The Drifters* of which more later. For Franco, NATO bases and rekindled tourism would represent much-needed status and income.

In the 1950s the French had invented a new tour route, Le Petit Tour, snaking down from France to Málaga by train and then along the Costabella (the name which preceded the Costa del Sol which we use today) to Gibraltar and over to Tangier and Marrakech. By then, however, civilian flights could land at an airstrip between Málaga and Torremolinos, and some celebrity press coverage led to the arrival of the first wealthy Americans. The website 'Memories of Torremolinos' contains a list of the rich and famous who visited in those early postwar years:

Rita Hayworth, Graham Green, Ava Gardner, Grace Kelly were among the celebrities to visit in the 1950s. Brigitte Bardot appeared in a film partly made in Torremolinos: 'Les bijoutiers du Clair de Lune'. Apparently the locals of La Carihuela were unhappy that she was behaving as Gala had almost thirty years before, sunbathing topless, and they wrote a letter of complaint to the Mayor of Málaga, who publicly called for Bardot to be deported due to her 'immoral behaviour and attitude.' One local resident was unhappy for a different reason: Rafael de la Fuente worked at Santa Clara and had to turn her away from the hotel as it was full.

Luxury hotels like nothing the resort had seen before began to be built. The first to open, on 31 May 1959, was the Hotel Pez Espada right behind La Carihuela beach. Its design introduced the concept of sets of colours, textures, wavy lines, etc. Two grand staircases in the lobby set the appearance of the main facade, characterized by a semi-cylindrical body. On the upper floors, the rooms are distributed asymmetrically on both sides of the gallery. In the six years before Pez Espada opened, six hotels were established; in the six years following, about fifty-five.

Other celebrities were to follow as the hotel provision expanded: Viviene Leigh and Sir Laurence Olivier, Marlon Brando, Elizabeth Taylor, Diana Dors, Juan Peron, Ingrid Bergman, Michele Morgan, Duke and Duchess of Windsor, King of Saudi Arabia Ibn Saud Abdel-Azis, Greta Garbo, Bobby Moore, Keith Richards, Boris Karloff, Sean Connery, Anita Ekberg, Judy Garland, Dino de Laurentis, Henri Charriere, George C. Scott, Sophia Loren . . .

Many films were made in the surrounding area, mainly Spanish and French but some English language ones. Dirk Bogarde and John Mills appeared in the *The Singer Not the Song*, filmed in Alhaurín in 1961. Frank Sinatra stayed in 1964 while filming *Von Ryan's Express* in El Chorro, a dramatic gorge north west of Málaga. Anthony Quinn and George Segal visited in 1966, filming scenes from *Lost Command* and using Málaga port as a location, while most of the film was shot in Almería. Raquel Welch visited in 1967 when filming *Fathom*. The film *Hard Contract* was shot in Torremolinos in 1969 with James Coburn, Lee Remick and Lilli Palmer.

Frank Sinatra is one celebrity who did not have fond memories of staying at the Pez Espada. He was staying at the hotel during filming of the final sequence of *Von Ryan's Express* and planned on spending an evening with a Cuban actress Ondina Canibano when a press photographer took their picture. There was an altercation with Sinatra's bodyguards which ended with the

photographer being taken away by the police who then wanted
to interview Sinatra as a witness. He blocked himself in his room
and the police were persuaded to let him complete filming first.
A couple of days later they came back for their statement and
took him off to the police station. Sinatra was not best pleased,
reacted badly and was then fined 25,000 pesetas. Allegedly he
vowed never to return to 'this [expletive deleted] country'.

Meanwhile a different type of tourist, still probably regarding
themselves a bit as pioneers, began to arrive. The youth and
diversity of this new population was captured in the novel *The
Drifters* by James A. Michener. The first six chapters introduce
the characters of the title one by one: Joe (twenty), a US draft
dodger; Britta (eighteen), a Norwegian who comes on holiday for
two weeks and stays; Monica (eighteen), the daughter of a British
colonial officer in a fictitious African country; Cato, a university
drop-out and the son of a US church minister; Yigal, ex-Israeli
army, the son of a college dean in Haifa – his British grandfather
suggested spending some time away; finally, Gretchen (nineteen)
a political intern in the USA who decides to go to France where
she buys a yellow VW camper van and travels to Torremolinos.
Michener aims to capture the new breed of young single traveller
(or tourist?) which was discovering the world beyond their home
confines in a new era of post-war affluence. Torremolinos had
become a magnet for them, just like Santa Clara appears to have
been a haven for the unconventional before the Civil war, now
the whole of the expanding Torremolinos was, to some, a 'hippy
hangout'. Bars, restaurants and cheap accommodation had sprung
up everywhere, while the tower block hotels of the coming mass
tourism were also in development. The latter may have done for
the former: hippies were never that good for the bank balance.
One report online pinpoints the summer of 1971 (coincidentally
the year *The Drifters* was first published) as the flashpoint. This
'den of iniquity', this refuge of druggies and homosexuals had,
amazingly, flourished under the noses of Franco's repressive,

Catholic Spain. One night in June police swooped and arrested over one hundred people, mainly foreigners, including many gays. Some clubs and bars were closed. Perhaps the reason was more economic than moral: the age of the package tourist had arrived. Those who had invested in the new hotel complexes wanted the best return on their money and low-spending 'drifters' and others were in the way.

In her autobiography published in 2007, Patricia Robins (Claire Lorrimer) writes:

> It is impossible to people arriving today in the huge skyscraper burger bar English pub environment of Torremolinos to imagine the peaceful isolation of that tiny part of the coast when my mother took us with our governess to holiday there three Easters in a row in the early 1930s.
>
> [She goes on to say] The orchards and olive groves along the road from Gibraltar to Málaga gave way to a wide coast road and then a motorway, and the golden sands were buried beneath beach cafés, sun umbrellas and lounge chairs. Torremolinos became all but a city of skyscrapers and Santa Clara, our hacienda, no longer exists. However the population must have welcomed the many new vast openings for employment and the huge influx of wealth from the tourists that has ensued.

She has a point, and it is not only the local population which will have welcomed the skyscraper hotels. If you were a wage-earning worker with limited leisure time from a cold north European country then two weeks in the sun in a place like Torremolinos was a reward you may have saved all year to obtain: your bit of paradise.

In 1961 a total of 300,000 international tourists used Málaga airport. The boom had really started, not only on the Costa del Sol, but along much of Spain's beautiful coastline; the peaceful isolation Robins and her family were fortunate enough to enjoy:

natural beauty, simplicity, absence of modern pressures, absence of crowds were gone, only to be identified elsewhere in the world by new generations of travel writers always seeking a new 'paradise'.

In truth, when George bought Santa Clara he and Annie were seeking that exclusivity and he enhanced the natural beauty he discovered. Despite her early death, he returned from his duty in the First World War with a new religious vision which compelled him to share his wealth with the local people and his home with his staff, who in turn were able to share it with those early guests. It is to the credit of the modern citizens of Torremolinos that they still wish to celebrate his contribution to their success.

APPENDIX I

Mercedes Beautell
Memories from Her Youth at Santa Clara

Mercedes was one of the four children of Margaret Beautell (née Horn) who ran the hotel from 1928, handing over to her older daughter Nancy who ran it with Mark Hawker up until the Spanish Civil War. Mercedes will have been about seventeen when she arrived at Santa Clara. She is writing in 2007 in her old age.

Mercedes (to the right) in 1930.
Courtesy Serra Hamilton Collection

The translation by the author is followed by the original Spanish:

> I am sitting looking at my bare feet – how ugly they are! – and thinking of far off times – how pretty they were then!! Today is a lovely day and I have come out onto the terrace to let the sun get at my bare legs (no stockings), so white, they are not pretty to look at. They look quite disagreeable and I began to think of so many things.
>
> I am old, it pains me to say I am old because I don't think of

myself as old but with a great yearning to live! The desire to know what's going on in this life of ours where so many things happen and there seems to be so much hatred.

I would love it if the whole world could remember their youth like I can. What a simple and marvellous life!

To think of a quiet little beach! That's now a luxury but in my day it was normal.

What a lovely place it was when we (my mother, brothers and I) arrived in Torremolinos in 1928. I know that it could not always be like that but for me and my family we had arrived in heaven!

Our life in 'Santa Clara' could never be repeated, it was unique! To wake up with the divine sun over a blue sea; it needs to be seen day after day to know how wonderful it was. In the years that I am talking about life was so simple and marvellous. I think it must have been like life in the Garden of Eden.

On hot days and nights we had the luck to be able to take our camp beds outside under climbers and creepers, beautiful creepers, full of blue flowers and we would sleep like that my mother, my brother Ed and me. Early in the morning we would see the lovely gardeners going about their work which included picking carnations to send, to be honest, I don't know where.

I often think of those marvellous gardeners- what must they have thought of this foreign family who arrived there and stayed. They were such lovely people, always ready to help us.

Santa Clara was, in reality, the property of an English gentleman who had bought it with the idea of bringing his (ill) wife who the doctors in London had sent to a mild climate. He set up this bungalow with such good taste, a big dining room since he intended to have guests, and plenty of them. It was all finished so well and the furniture was fabulous. But the thing he least expected happened, his wife died before they were able to enjoy this marvel!

For poor Major Langworthy it was a mortal blow and in reality he did not believe that his beloved wife had passed on to a better life (this thing about a better life is something we still don't know about, if you'll forgive me saying!).

So he turned a little . . . I wouldn't say mad, not that, because in those days he gave me tennis lessons.

He could see my great love for the game and with his great patience, every morning he was waiting for me on the tennis court with a big basket of 200 balls and with all his great kindness he taught me to hold the racquet well and I managed to play (not Wimbledon standard) but well enough to win matches and to enjoy this marvellous sport. The sad thing for me was when the poor major, playing with some friends, stood on some rough ground and his days as a tennis player came to an end as he had damaged the ligaments in his leg and as his religious beliefs did not allow him to believe in illness (nor in doctors) – that's to say he called it 'right thinking'; there is no illness only what one thinks since God only desires the good from everyone and if there is a pain it is because our human-ness thinks so. I could tell quite a few amusing tales about this but I will tell just two.

We had stayed in Santa Clara, my mother and I since through the friendship we had with Mr Boyer (not the minister but the man who was at that time the chief of General Motors) and a stroke of luck he offered work to my brother Eduardo and to my sister Nancy and they went to Madrid and when what I'm going to tell you happened there was only my mother, her only sister (who was English) and me at Santa Clara.

We received news that Eduardo was in hospital with peritonitis. Poor Mamá! She had to go on the first train that left that night. Major Langworthy of course, the good major, found out and came at once to our humble little home (these days it would be called an apartment). Since he was so well received by everybody – I've never known anybody like him – he came in and said, Mrs Beautell, we must do an 'absent treatment' we sat round the table and he began to pray with great devotion. I was young then and it seemed very strange to me and beyond my understanding, so much so that I was dying to laugh and as it was going on so long and my mother had to catch the train we began to get restless. But not the major. He bade farewell to Mamá saying, 'All will be well'. And it was! My brother who was quite ill became better straight away.

The other anecdote which I will tell you is really funny.

Every morning a certain Miguelín would come with his little donkey. The donkey was loaded with the best of things! Grapes in huge bunches still with the morning dew on them. Miguelin was always greeted with joy, not just because he brought the best with him but because he was so natural and kind. The wonderful muscatel grapes which were sold in those days cost 10 or 20 cents!

Well, it so happened Miguelito did not appear for a few days and when he came back he told us that someone had mugged him for what little he had and they had given him a fine blow to the head which left him knocked out for a few days. The day he came back, the major also found out he had also been missing (the colonel [*sic*] was vegetarian and obviously he always bought fruit from Miguel). We were all sitting round Miguel with him telling us about his misfortune, sporting a black eye and a lump still visible on his head but my beloved Major Langworthy wanted to convince him that what had happened to him was because it was not right thinking but wrong thinking and that nothing had actually happened to him. Miguelín's face was a picture! He said, 'But, sir, and this lump on my head, how did it get there?'

All these little funny things leave me thinking how Major Langworthy was a unique person and a saint and I say saint because you don't get people like him anymore.

With his fortune could have lived like a lord but he was happy with his life giving most of what he had to his little village. When he died he gave everything to his faithful gardeners who had looked after him throughout his life, not that he needed much looking after, he asked for so little.

What wonderful memories of such a person. I still think that in this great big world there are people like him but what I most like about him is that only a few of us knew what he was like, of course in those days there was no press or radio etc. etc, these days in no time at all everyone knows about everything, the good and the bad.

One day I will carry on with my stories from those happy days of my youth. And I say happy since I think that these days what we called happy, today they would say it was a drag! Boring!

But thank God, I have lived through these times without upset and with great happiness.

(1928–33)
(Author's translation)

* * *

Estoy sentada viendo mis pies desnudos. ¡qué feos son!..y pensar en los tiempos lejanos ¡que eran tan bonitos!! Hoy, un día precioso y salí a la terraza para tomar el sol en las piernas (para no usar medias)-pues piernas desnudas blancas francamente resultan bastante desagradables – y empecé en pensar en tantas cosas.

Soy vieja – me da una pena decir vieja, pues no me encuentro vieja, sino con unas ganas de vivir! Unas ganas de saber lo que está pasando en esta vida nuestra donde tantas cosas pasan y donde tanto odio parece haber.

Me encantaría si todo el mundo se acordasen de su juventud como you ¡Que vida tan sencilla y maravillosa!

¡Pensar en una playa pequeña y solitaria! Eso es ya un lujo, pero en mis tiempos era normal.

Qué pueblo más encantador cuando nosotros (mi madre, hermanos y yo) llegamos en Torremolinos en el año 1928. Comprendo que no todo podía seguir así pero para mí y mi familia habíamos llegado al cielo!!

Nuestra vida en 'Santa Clara' nunca se podrá repetir, ¡era única! Despertarte con el sol divino sobre un mar azul, esto hay que verlo día tras día para saber lo divino que es. En los años de

los cuales me refiero, la vida era tan maravillosa y sencilla. Yo
creo que era como la vida en el Edén.

Los días y noches de calor teníamos la suerte de poder sacar
nuestros 'catres' bajo una enredadera preciosa con ramos de flores
azules y así dormíamos mi madre, mi hermano Ed y yo. Temprano
por la mañana veíamos a los simpáticos jardineros que iban a
sus faenas que era coger los claveles para enviar, en esos tiempos
francamente, no sé donde.

Muchas veces pienso en estos maravillosos jardineros – que
pensarían en esta familia extranjera que llegaron ahi y se quedaron.
Eran tan buena gente y siempre con ganas de ayudarnos.

La finca de 'Santa Clara', en realidad era de un señor inglés que
lo había comprador con la idea de traer a su mujer (enferma) y que
los médicos de Londres mandaron a un clima suave. Él monto ese
bungalow con tanto gusto, un comedor grande, pues el pensaba
tener invitados – y muchos. Todod estaba amueblado con mucho
gusto, pues los muebles eran algunos de maravilla. Pero pasó lo
que nunca se esperó, su mujer antes de disfrutar de esta maravilla,
se murió!

Para el pobre Major Langworthy fue un golpe mortal y no creía
que en realidad su querida esposa había pasado a mejor vida (esto
de mejor vida todavía no lo sabemos con perdón!).

Entonces se volvió un poco...no diría loco, pues de eso nada
porque aquel en entonces él me daba clases de tennis.

Él veía mi gran afición y con toda su gran paciencia, todas las
mañanas me esperaba en el campo de tennis con un gran cesto con
200 pelotas, y con toda su gran bondad, me ensañaba a coger la
raqueta bien, y llegué a poder jugar (no de Wimbledon) pero si a
poder ganar partidos y a poder gozar de este juego maravilloso. La
pena fue mía cuando al pobre major jugando con unos amigos pisó
mal algún terreno y su vida de tenista terminó pues los ligamentos
de su pierna sufrieron daños y como el por su religion no creía en el
mal (o en los médicos) – o sea el lo llamaba 'right thinking' en esto,
no hay mal sino lo que uno piensa, pues Dios no quiere sino el bien

de todos y si hay un dolor es porque nuestra humanidad lo piensa así. Sobre esto podía contra varias anécdotas francamente saladas, pero contaré solamente dos.

Nos habíamos quedado en Sta. Clara, my madre y yo pues con mucha suerte y por la Amistad que tuvimos com Mr Boyer (no el ministro sino en aquel entonces el Jefe de General Motors, él ofreció trabajo a mi hermano Eduardo y a mi hermana Nancy, y ellos claro se fueron a Madrid y cuando ocurrió lo que voy a contas estábamos solamente mi madre, la única hermana de mi madre (inglesa) y yo.

Pues recibimos la noticia de que Eduardo estaba ingresado en el hospital pues tenia peritonitis. Pobre mamá! Tenía que salir en el primer tren que salía de noche. M. Langworthy, claro, el bueno del major, se enteró y vino en seguida a nuestro pequeño y humilde hogar (hoy en dia se llamaría apartamento). Y como era tan bien recibido por todos, pues como él nunca he conocido a nadie, entró y dijo, Mrs Beautell, hay que hacer un 'absent treatment', nos sentamos alrededor de la mesa y el con mucha devoción empezó a rezar. Yo era joven en aquel entonces y todo me parecía rarífico y fuera de mis entendimientos, tanto así que me daban ganas de reir y además como la cosa se largaba tanto y mi madre tenía que coger el tren, se notaba una sensación de nerviosismo. Pero no por parte del major. Se despidió de mama diciendo 'todo irá bien'. Y así fue! Mi hermano que estuvo bastante grave mejoró enseguida.

La otra anecdota que cuento es realmente salada. Venía todas las mañanas con su pequeño burro un tal Miguelín. El burro venía cargado de lo mejor! Uvas en grandes racimos todavía con el rocío de la mañana. A Miguel siempre lo recibíamos con alegría pues no solamente traía lo major, sino que era tan sencillo y simpatico, las maravillosas uvas Mostatel en aquella época se vendían a real o 20 céntimos!

Pues resultó que faltó Miguelito durante varios días y cuando llegó nos contó que alguien le había atracado para quitarle lo poco que tenía y le habían dado un buen golpe en la cabeza que lo dejó

K.O. durante varios días. El día que regresó estaba el major que también se había enterado de la falta de Miguelín (el coronel era vegetariano y claro la fruta siempre se compraba a M.). Estábamos todos alrededor de M. Y el contándonos su desgracia además con un ojo bastante en tinta y un chichón todavía visible en su cabeza.

Pero mi querido major Langworthy quiso convencerle de que le había pasado era porque no era el right thinking sino el wrong thinking y que nada de eso había pasado. La cara de Miguelín era un poema! Y dijo, pero señor, y este bulto en la cabeza, por qué me ha salido?

Sobre todas estas pequeñas y divertidas cosas siempre me queda un pensamiento y es que major Langworthy era una persons única y un santo, y digo santo porque personas como él ya ni se dan.

El con su fortuna, podría haber vivido como hoy en día viven los potentados, pero él fue feliz con su vida dando lo mejor que el tenía a su pequeño pueblo.

Al morir dejo todo a sus fieles jardineros que durante su vida lo habían cuidado, y poco cuidado necesito el pues pedía de lo poco, lo menos.

Que recuerdos tan maravillosos de una persona así. – si, todavía creo que por este gran mundo hay personas como él, pero de él lo que me encanta es que solamnete pocos sabíamos como era, claro en aquellos tiempos no había la prensa, radio, etc etc, de hoy en día que al poco tiempo, todo el mundo sabe de todo y de todos, lo bueno y lo malo.

Algun día seguiré mis relatos de aquellos años felices de mi juventud. Y yo digo felices pues creo que hoy en día lo que llamábamos felices, hoy por hoy dirían que rollo! Que aburrimiento!

Pero yo gracias a Dios he vivido todos estos años sin traumas y con mucha felicitad.

(1928–33)
(Original Spanish text)

APPENDIX II

Extracts from 'El Indolente'
by Luis Cernuda (1902–1963)

'El Indolente' is one of three short stories (*Tres Narraciones*) first published in 1958 in Buenos Aires, though Cernuda gives 1929 as the date he wrote 'El Indolente' in the edition I possess, published by Seix Barral in Barcelona in 1974. The edition states that these three stories are the only ones written by Cernuda who was a poet and a member of the 'Generation of '27' who stayed at Santa Clara along with other writers and artists

Photo: Luis Cernuda (centre), Lorca (left), Aleixandre (right). Origin unknown.

In 'El Indolente', Torremolinos becomes 'Sansueña' and 'Don Míster' is undoubtedly based on George Langworthy, though details such as his age are changed. This story has a dreamlike quality in which the fictional Englishman resolves to rescue from the sea an ancient statue with the help of three characters called Aire, Guitarra and Olvido (Air, Guitar and Oblivion) but Aire dies on the night of the attempt. Cernuda subscribed to surrealism, and the themes he develops as the story goes on are ones that he also addresses in his poetry rather than issues related to George.

The extracts below set the scene and offer descriptions of the man and his home. The original Spanish follows the English translation by the author.

Extracts from 'El Indolente' or 'The Languorous One':

> Sansueña is a place on the coast, by the clear, deep, southern sea. A town of light, if there is such a thing, all white, green and blue, with its olive trees, its black and white poplars and that shock of prickly pears at the foot of a reddish crag . . .
>
> In Sansueña the eyes open to a pure light and the chest breathes in fragrant air. No yearning pains the heart because desire has died in the beauty of living; of living like things live: with a passionate silence. Peace has made its home where those men sleep sheltered from the sun. And although dawn wakes them, going in their boats to tend to the nets, back with the catch by midday, peace reigns throughout the day as well; a vibrant, sonorous, luminous peace. If ever I am lost, come and find me in Sansueña.
>
> Don Míster, as they called him, knew this very well. His real name doesn't matter, but that was their name for the Englishman who, years before, had bought that roomy house standing proud amongst the crags. It was surrounded by a sloping garden whose terraces ended at the sea, on the rocks that the water had been hollowing out; rocks where night and day the the sleepless voice of the waves made itself heard, the surf breaking to leave the greenish sheen of the sea streaked with pearls of foam, as if the roses in bloom overhead amongst the palm trees in the garden beds, were raining down, petal by petal, scorched by the summer heat.
>
> In one of the ground floor rooms of the house, on some hides laid out on the floor, don Míster slept next to the grille of a window that I never saw closed neither in summer nor in winter, whether the sun shone or the wind whistled through. He could not go to

sleep unless he could hear the lullaby of the sea, drawing him to dream his boyhood dreams.

'Boy' is exactly what the people of Sansueña called him. When an Andalusian speaks to someone, there are only two ways: boy or granddad. There a man can be 'boy' till he is forty, fifty, even older. Then in a single sad moment they stop regarding us as boys and see us as granddads. 'Boy, get out of here, you're in my way,' calmly says some rider on a donkey to the man on foot who hasn't seen him. 'Grandad, keep close to the wall so's I won't hit you,' says the same rider if the man on foot is older, raising his voice because he presumes that if he's not exactly senile at least the poor man will be deaf.

The character I am talking about today still fell into the first category: 'boy'. That's what they sometimes genially called him, although at other times it would be Don Míster, Míster Inglés or simply the Englishman. With his dark hair and his smiling face he didn't fit the usual look of his race. Nonetheless, naked or half-dressed he took on the typical gracelessness of his countrymen who only acquire their proverbial elegance and poise when they put on their city suits . . .

Even now I see his at dusk, dressed as usual in white, a blue kerchief knotted carelessly below the open collar of his shirt, strolling along the paths of his seaside garden. Sometimes he picks up the leaves that the breeze has blown onto the gravel, other times he fixes his eyes on the immense horizon, breathing in the air heavy with the scent of the jasmines and the magnolias. There was something in the way his chest rose and fell in that deep intake of breath, a kind of challenge, as if to say: who can take away this essential, subtle pleasure of being nothing, of knowing nothing, of expecting nothing? The perfume of the air, entering his lungs, responded to his quiet, reserved spirit with a yes from the earth, also silent and reserved. The earth and the man were in accord. Who could ask for more?

After wandering through the flower-lined paths of the garden

we sat on the whitewashed benches of the look-out set on an
outcrop over the sea. On one side, between the leaves of a climbing
plant, its blue bellflowers open, the beach below stretched out,
vast and empty. Further away could be seen the first houses of
the village, white, with pink roofs and green shutters like doves
wearing ribbons that a lover has sent his beloved in a wicker tray.
If the day was clear, and that dust that gives vision a quivering
uncertain feeling, the mountains of Africa would rise up, strangely
close, pin-point sharp yet unreal.

'I envy you,' I said to Don Míster one of these evenings. 'You
don't have the things that other people think are the necessities
of life, like a radio, a telephone or newspapers. Instead you have
everything that people think is superfluous, from the flowers and
the air to solitude. Who would be you!' I added with a sigh.

'Well, it's simple,' he replied. 'Don't go to the city. Nobody
obliges you to. Do you need to work to earn a living? In these trees
there is fruit all year round. Anyone here will give you a little bread
out of charity. Remember the pleas of the beggars with bare feet and
eyes of jet who go around here from door to door asking for bread.'

As he spoke, he rubbed a sprig of basil between his fingers,
breathing in the aroma that impregnated his skin, then he added:

'In this house, although it no longer belongs to me, you will
never be short of a place to rest.'

I remembered that in truth, the house was no longer his. His
family, over there in England, had ended up worrying about how
he spent his money despite the respect that some of them professed
for what we could call the right to be extravagant; an essential right
for life, and one forgotten by the old French revolutionaries when
they proclaimed their decalogue.

His relatives had let him live the way he wanted, until one day
they learned that he paid everyone in Sansueña five pesetas a day
to listen for an hour to him reading out loud various verses from
the Bible. Since those folk barely earned a peseta a day for nine
or ten hours of hard work, soon work was put to one side and the

audience soon matched the number of people in the village, quickly shrinking Don Míster's supply of cash.

I suspected that he had no intention, with his readings, of making converts, nor of liberating victims from the Papist tyranny, but that that was the most considerate way that he could find to justify his generosity towards those poor people. Nor do I think that he wanted to educate their literary tastes, opening their eyes to the beauty of the divine text, because if there are not many that I have found with such rich and expressive language there are also few that I know with less inclination to books and reading. He would have laboured in vain.

His relatives were not so cruel as to deprive Don Míster of his liberty, obliging him to return to a land, a society and a climate that he detested. What they did do was to put him under a kind of guardianship, like a child, despite his forty-odd years. His house was divided into sections and these, with the exception of one reserved for him, were rented out to foreigners who turned up there from remote climates, like migrating birds, to forget, between the sea and the sky, in a beautiful corner of the world, their irritating civilisation.

The building was extremely spacious and these unavoidable neighbours never caused any disturbance. At most, during the night-time, when it was already late, and if we were crossing the patio on the way up from the beach, we might hear a whisper or a kiss reaching our ears from behind the shutters left half open because of the heat. No doubt some foreigner, man or woman, was yielding to love with one of the young people of Sansueña. Since these foreigners were rich and generous (qualities which are rarely found in the same person), pleasure and profit rained down on the golden local youth.

How beautiful were those creatures! In truth, sometimes the woman would have graced this earth for as little as fifteen years and would soon lose the purity of adolescence. But deep down she kept an instinctive notion of beauty, in accordance with which her many descendants would be conceived and shaped. The young men, skinny and hairless, could keep their youthful bearing for longer until, as if they were made of wood and not flesh, their bodies became wrinkled and knotted under their patched clean clothes. Right from childhood they were as exquisite as a flower and as delicious as a fruit. I would watch them laugh and run down on the beach, then stop suddenly, turning their cheeky, teasing faces upwards, and shout to me: 'Money! Money!' They assumed that I was a foreigner as well and deployed the only word of my supposed language that they had learned, interestingly. To me of all people, who was as Andalusian as them if not more so, and who, although I may have slaved away in those worlds, had been born in the very heart of Andalusia.

(Author's translation)

* * *

Sansueña es un pueblo ribereño en el mar del sur, transparente y profundo. Un pueblo claro si los hay, todo blanco, verde y azul, con sus olivos, sus chopos y sus álamos y su golpe aquel de chumberas, al pie de una peña rojiza . . .

En Sansueña los ojos se abren a una luz pura y el pecho respira un aire oloroso. Ningún deseo duele al corazón, porque el deseo ha muerto en la beatitud de vivir; de vivir como viven las cosas: con silencio apasionado. La paz ha hecho su morada bajo los sombrajos donde duermen estos hombres. Y aunque el amanecer les despierte, yendo en sus barcas a tender las redes, a mediodía retiradas con el copo, también durante el día reina la paz; una paz militante, sonora y luminosa. Si alguna vez me pierdo, que vengan a buscarme aquí, a Sansueña.

Bien sabía esto Don Míster como llamaban (su verdadero nombre no hace al caso) todos al inglés que años atras compró aquella casa espaciosa, erguida entre las peñas. La rodeaba un jardín en pendiente cuyas terrazas morían junto al mar, sobre las rocas que el agua había ido socavando; rocas donde día y noche resonaban las olas con voz insomne, rompiendo su cresta de espuma, para dejar luego la piel verdosa del mar estriada de copos nacarados, como si las rosas abiertas arriba entre palmeras, en los arriates del jardín, lloviesen, deshechas y consumidas de ardor bajo la calma estival.

En una de las habitaciones bajas de la casa, sobre unas pieles tendidas en el suelo, dormía Don Míster, junto a la reja de una ventana que nunca vi cerrada, fuese invierno or verano, brillara el sol o azotara el vendoval. No podia conciliar el sueño si en sus oídos no cantaba la nana del mar, acunando sus fantasías de niño viejo.

Niño le llamaban precisamente las gentes de Sansueña. Para el andaluz, cuando interpela a alguien, sólo dos términos hay, y son éstos: niño o abuelo. Allá puede uno ser niño hasta los cuarenta, cincuenta y aún más. Luego, de un salto brusco y triste, dejan de considerarnos como niños para mirarnos como abuelos. <<Niño, quítate de ahí, que me haces sombre>>, dice parsimonioso quien va caminando, jinete sobre un borrico, al peatón que no le ha visto. <<Abuelo,arrímese a la pared , no vaya a chocarle>>, dice el mismo jinete si el peatón es hombre mayor, dando entonces más brío a la voz, porque presume que la edad, si no chocho, al menos habrá dejado sordo al pobre.

En esta categoría de niño figuraba todavía el personaje de quien hoy me propongo hablar. Así le llamaban campechanamente a veces, aunque otras fuese Don Míster, Míster Inglés o bien el Inglés a secas. Con pelo negro y cara sonriente, desmentía la estampa tradicional de la raza. Sin embargo, al verle desnudo o a medio vestir, guardaba el desgarbo típico de sus compatriotas, quienes sólo al endosar el traje urbano convierten en esbeltez las líneas escuetas, adquiriendo su prestancia y buen porte proverbiales....

Aún le veo a la caída de la tarde, vestido como solía de blanco, con un pañuelo azul anudado al desgaire bajo el cuello abierto de la camisa, paseando por los senderos de su jardín marino. Unas veces recoge las hojas que la brisa dejó caer sobre la grava, otras laza los ojos para abarcar el horizonte inmenso, aspirando luego el aire lleno de perfume de los jazmines y de las magnolias. Había en su gesto, al encoger y dilatar el pecho en aquella ancha respiración, una especie de reto, como si dijera: ¿quien me puede quitar este gozo elemental y sutil de no ser nada , de no saber nada, de no esperar nada? El perfume del aire, entrando por sus pulmones , respondía a su espíritu reservado y silencioso con un sí, tambien reservado y silencioso, de la tierra. La tierra y él estaban de acuerdo.¿Podía pedirse algo más?

Despues de recorrer las veredas floridas del jardín nos sentábamos en los bancos encalados del balconcillo, abierto en un repecho sobre el mar. A un lado, entre las hojas de la enredadera, abiertas sus campanillas azules, se veía la playa alargarse abajo, vasta y solitaria. Más lejos aparecían las primeras casas del pueblo, blancas, de tejados rosas y postigos verdes, como palomas adornadas con cintas que un enamorado enviara a su amor dentro de un canastillo. Si el día era claro y se disipaba la niebla luminosa del sur, ese polvo sutil que hace trémula e incierta la vision tal en un sueño, podían verse las montañas de África, aceradas e irreales, brotar extrañamente cerca.

-Le envidio-dije yo a Don Míster una de esas tardes-. Carece usted de lo que la gente considera como necesario para vivir, ya sea aparato de radio, teléfono o periódicos. Tiene en cambio todo lo que hoy se considera superfluo, desde las flores y el aire hasta la soledad. ¡Quien fuera usted!-añadí con un suspiro.

-Pues es bien fácil-me respondió-. No vuelva a la capital. Nadie le obliga a ello. ¿Tiene necesidad de trabajar para ganarse la vida? En esos árboles hay fruta todo el año. Un poco de pan cualquiera suele darlo aquí como limosna. Recuerde la súplica de los mendiguillos con pies descalzos y ojos de azabache que van por ahí de puerta en puerta pidiendo un pedazo de pan.

Acariciaba entretanto, al hablar así, las hojas de una mata de albahaca, y aspirando el aroma de que se habían impregnado sus dedos, añadió luego:

-En esta casa, aunque ya no es mía, nunca le faltará un rincón donde echarse a decansar.

Recordé que en efecto la casa no era suya. Su famila, allá

en Inglaterra, había acabado por inquietarse de cómo gastaba el dinero, a pesar del respeto profesado por algunas de aquellas gentes a lo que pudiéramos llamar el derecho a la extravagancia; derecho imprescindible para la vida y olvidado por los viejos revolucionarios franceses al promular su decálogo.

Los parientes le habían dejado vivir a su gusto, hasta que un buen día supieron que pagaba a cada vecino de Sansueña cinco pesetas diarias por escuchar durante una hora la lectura que en voz alta les hacía de varios versículos de la Biblia. Como aquellas gentes del pueblo apenas si obtenían una peseta de jornal por nueve o diez horas de esfuerzo agotador, pronto el trabajo se dejó a un lado y el grupo de oyentes llegó a equivaler al número de vecinos, descendiendo en proporcion rápida el capital de Don Míster.

Sospechaba yo que éste no pretendió con tales lecturas hacer prosélitos del libre examen ni libertar víctimas de la tiranía papista, sino que ésa fue la forma más delicada que hallo para justificar su generosidad con aquellas pobres gentes. Ni siquiera cabía pensar que quiso educar sus gustos literarios, abriéndoles los ojos a la hermosura del texto divino, porque si bien pocos he hallado con lenguaje tan rico y expresivo como éstos, pocos también conozco con menos inclinación a la lectura y a los libros. Hubiera sido pena perdida.

No fueron tan crueles los parientes en cuestión como privar a Don Míster de su libertad, obligándole a regresar a una tierra, una sociedad y un clima que detestaba. Le pusieron, eso sí, en tutela como a un chico, a pesar de sus cuarenta años corridos. Su casa fue dividida en departamentos, y éstos, con excepción de uno reservado para él mismo, alquilados a extranjeros que acudían allí desde climas remotos, como aves migratorias, para olvidar entre el cielo y el mar, en un rincón bello del mundo, una civilización enojosa.

El edificio era espacioso en extremo y estos vecinos forzosos no molestaban nunca. Apenas si por la noche, ya tarde, cuando subiendo desde la playa cruzábamos el patio, se oía a veces un susurro o un beso, que llegaban a nuestros oídos a través de los postigos entreabiertos a cause del calor. Sin duda alguien, extranjero o extranjera, estaba sacrificando al amor acompañado por uno de los hijos de Sansueña. Como estos extranjeros eran ricos y generosos (cualidades que raramente van juntas), placer y provecho llovían sobre la dorada juventud local.

¡Qué hermosas eran aquellas criaturas! Verdad es que a veces la mujer sólo tenía la gracia de los quince años, y que pronto perdía las líneas puras de la adolescencia. Mas en su entraña guardaba un arquetipo instintivo de hermosura, con arreglo al cual era concebida y formada su descendencia numerosa. El hombre, glabro y cenceño, podia conservar más tiempo el porte juvenil, hasta que, como si fuese de madera, y no de carne, su cuerpo quedaba arrugado y nudoso bajo los limpios vestidos remendados. De niños, de muchachos, eran exquisitos como una flor y sabrosos como un fruto. Abajo en la playa los veía yo correr y reír, y alzando depronto las caras frescas y burlonas, pararse gritaándome: <<¡Money! ¡Money!>> Me suponían también extranjero y proferían la única palabra de mi supuesto lenguaje que habían aprendido interesadamente. A mí, que era tan andaluz como ellos, si no más, y que aunque hubiese azacaneado mis huesos por esos mundos, nací en el corazón mismo de Andalucía.'

(Original Spanish text)

APPENDIX III

Verbatim extract from the
Pall Mall Gazette of 24 May 1887

THE

PALL MALL GAZETTE

An Evening Newspaper and Review.

| No. 6921.—Vol. XLV. | *TUESDAY, MAY 24, 1887.* | *Price One Penny.* |

The Lady, the Lawyers, and the Public

We publish tomorrow, in convenient compass, in response to a widespread demand, the strange, true story of 'The Langworthy Marriage.' The interest which that 'ower true tale' has excited in 'all sorts and conditions of men' is a gratifying sign of the times. Beyond publishing the story from day to day and telling our readers how Mrs Langworthy may be helped, no personal appeal has been made, but already a sympathizing public has forwarded to this office subscriptions amounting to upwards of £1,300. This substantial earnest of the support which Mrs Langworthy may confidently reckon upon in her gallant and arduous struggle for justice, is a welcome and satisfactory indication of the healthy public interest that has been excited by the simple narrative which will now in a complete form find a much wider circle of readers in every part of the three kingdoms.

It would indeed have been a burning shame if wrongs such as those which it has been a painful duty to lay bare before the world, had elicited no answering response, especially from women. From the crowned woman on the throne who to-day celebrates her sixty-eighth birthday, down to the humblest member of her sex, they have all a deep interest in the fortunes of Mrs Langworthy. But we have to regret that in the great profession which has entered into the inheritance of the Knights Templars of former times, there have been less tangible manifestations of chivalry and generosity than in almost any other order in the State. Mr Langworthy, it is true, is a barrister but that is surely no reason why men of the bar should ignore his offences. The clergy, from the Bishop of the dioceses in which Mrs Langworthy laboured, down to the humblest local preacher, have contributed more of their scanty means than the wealthy and the learned profession, in some of whose most eminent members Mr Langworthy found the most efficient allies in the four years' war which he has waged against his unfortunate wife. If only to wipe off the stain which this case has left on the reputation of the English lawyers, it might have been thought that there is hardly a lawyer in the land who has read the story of the 'lie in the affidavit' who would not hasten to mark his indignation at such practices by contributing his guinea to enable their victim to baffle her persecutor. Possibly it has not occurred to them in that light, and the same may be the case with the other members of the legal profession, both on the bench and the bar. We cannot believe that the judges, who have throughout shown so clear an appreciation of the issues, will hesitate to show their hearty satisfaction that effective means have been employed to avert what would have been a black and burning blot upon the administration of English justice. No one who cares for the reputation of his country's courts, no one who wishes to maintain unimpaired the lofty traditions of English law, will be backward in furnishing the means whereby

Mrs Langworthy may baffle the machinations of her enemy and defy the malevolent iniquity which employs even the safeguards of justice as the most efficient of all the engines of oppression.

We confidently commend the story of a woman's wrongs of the law's delays, and of the advantages which wealth commands in our courts, to the attention of the country, and especially to those keepers of the ears of King Demos, the editors of our newspapers. As yet, with a few notable exceptions, they have hardly noticed the case. Yet it is no transcript from ancient history. It is a live fact of today. Miss Langworthy was examined by the Official receiver last Friday. Her mother is to be examined this week. The public examination will follow, when *The Times*, even to oblige Messrs Bircham, will not venture again to boycott Mrs Langworthy. Journalistic jealousy is surely out of place in a case such as this. If our contemporaries think that in anything or in all things we have done amiss, let them condemn us as they will, if, while they censure us, they arouse public attention to the evils which this case has brought to light. Neither can it be a matter of no concern to the keepers of the conscience of the public, ministers of religion, under whatever name they may be called, that so flagrant an outrage should go unnoticed, or that so excellent an opportunity for enforcing a great and much-needed moral lesson should pass by unimproved. For the Langworthy case but exhibits in an extreme form many of the evils which are eating into the heart of our modern civilization. There is the employment of wealth as a weapon to crush instead of a lever to raise; there is the prostitution of the forms of the law in order to defeat the ends of justice; there is above all, Selfishness, that Anti-Christ of all time, exalted into the Supreme law of life with its hideous concomitant of human sacrifice. It is the heathenism of our day made manifest, a horrible apocalypse of the vulgar, of brutal lust, and of ruthless avarice.

To witness these things and not to cry out against them, or at least energetically to do all that can be done to mark in practical fashion our abhorrence of them and of all who aid and

abet and justify such abominations, is to make ourselves partakers
in their iniquity. If no loud protest is raised against the cunning
incorporation of lies in affidavits; the judicious distribution of
knowledge which enable witnesses to evade inquiry; and the want
of information so that clerks can unknowingly make incorrect
statements, these methods will become part of the ordinary
appliances of litigation. From that to the wholesale purchase of
witnesses in the market-place at so much a head it is but a step,
nor, indeed can it be said to be a step downwards. For the Oriental
method is at least honest in its dishonesty and straightforward in its
perjury. But the use of lies in affidavits and the applications for delay
on the strength of statements made 'to the best of my information
and belief' by clerks uninformed of facts, are like the stab of the
stiletto compared with which the lies of the professional witness
in India are as 'the weapons of the warrior'. These are matters on
which the Incorporated Law Society must surely have something
to say before long. Something must be done to improve the ethics
of a profession when its respectable members can not only do these
things, but can justify then afterwards in calm reflection when the
facts are unveiled to the light of day. And the first thing to be done
is to let in the light, and let every honest man and woman see what
kind of work can go on unchecked in the Victorian era even in the
very year of the Jubilee.

APPENDIX IV

Extract from the *Black Horse Gazette*, July 1910

'A Motor Tour in France'
By Major G. Langworthy (late 7th Dgn. Gds.)
Copyright The Royal Dragoon Guards Collection, York Army Museum

Dear Mr Editor

I enclose a short account of a very pleasant tour I made in France last summer which may be of interest to the readers of the B.H.G., more especially as the early part of it was through a district not usually traversed:-

My wife and I had intended at first to motor direct from Málaga to France, but the roads were so bad, especially in Southern Spain, and the maps worse than useless, that we decided to send the chauffeur and motor, a 20-hp *Star*, by sea to Marseilles, and followed on later ourselves.

The French authorities gave us no trouble and in less than two hours after landing we had our licences etc. and were all ready for the road.

Our first destination was Nimes, but instead of taking the direct route to Arles through St Chamas we branched off to the north by Aix (Provence) and St Cannat to see the effects of the earthquake, which occurred a few weeks before our arrival.

The 20-hp Star, built in Wolverhampton. Courtesy of Remi Fernandez Campoy.

Saint Chamas, Lambese, and Salon were some of the villages we passed through, and all three had the appearance of having suffered a severe bombardment. Hardly a house had escaped without damage, and many were in absolute ruins. We took several photographs, one of which I enclose, and then rattled along at a good pace to Arles. The road being almost straight, level and of excellent surface.

Arles is not a prepossessing town, the streets being dirty and badly laid, and the children numerous and aggressive: to make matters worse, we lost our way, and had to return, all of which was not conducive to enjoyment or good temper. I mention this, as it was about the only place where we had any difficulty in finding our way, for in the Michellin guide all the routes are most carefully shewn and explained, plans being given of all the principal towns, so that we were able in most cases to find our way even without asking.

After passing down a beautiful avenue of plane trees for some miles, we reached Nimes at 6.30 p.m. and put up at the Hotel

Luxembourg. The place was en fete as some celebrated Spanish Toreros were performing the following day at a Bull Fight in the old Roman Amphitheatre, which is capable of accommodating 24,000 spectators.

If at any time a reader of this article should find himself stranded for a few days at Marseilles I would strongly recommend a run up to Nimes.

A few days later an early start was made for Carcassonne. The road was fairly flat all the way, and we kept up a steady 30 kilometres an hour: one of the greater charms of motoring, I think, is to listen to the gentle humming of the engine, and to feel the sense of power one has to control, by the slightest movement of the hand or foot the great forces that are moving one along.

Beziers, a picturesque old Roman town standing on a hill, soon came in sight and we stopped a few seconds to take a picture of it, and then speeding along reached Carcassone before dusk.

There is no doubt that Carcassonne was a fortress of great importance in medieval times. It has a double line of fortifications, which can be seen in the photograph. The outer line is nearly one mile in circumference and the inner about 1,200 yards with only two entrances: there are fifty round towers and a citadel, and it was considered one of the most complete and formidable fortifications of those days, and is still in a very good state of preservation.

We were now gradually approaching the Pyrenees and after leaving Carcassonne the character of the country rapidly changed, for, in place of level roads, we had to negotiate some stiffish hills. The faithful Star, however, never failed us, but, making light of them all, soon brought us to Pamiers where we stopped to lunch. After crossing the River Ariege we began a real stiff ascent with very sharp turns. The view on reaching the top was truly glorious and well worth the short halt we made.

Coasting downhill for a few miles brought us quickly to Mas D'Azil, a large natural tunnel through which the main road runs with the river alongside. The photograph shows our car at the entrance.

The tunnel is in some places quite 100 yards wide and there are many curves throughout its length. It is necessary to light the lamps owing to the dense darkness, as one enters: the effect is most weird, hearing the roaring of the river, yet seeing nothing but the glare of the acetylene lamps reflected, first on one wall and then on the other, as the motor slowly wends its way around the sharp curves. Emerging into daylight once more, we soon reached St Girons, where the scenery had much the resemblance to that of the Thames Valley.

Although a little out of the way it well worthwhile to take the route by Mazeres and Roquefort: it is but a few miles further but the scenery is superb, changing constantly as one travels for a space along the banks of the river, again for a moment enjoying the shade of small plantation, and then gradually rising by easy gradients to higher ground, where one could see the whole valley spread out before one's eyes.

During the whole tour there was nothing to equal those few miles for beautiful and varying landscape.

Time was now getting short if we wished to arrive at Tarbes, our next halt, before dusk. We had some 86 kilometres still to cover, but keeping up a steady average, as the road was fairly straight, wide and clear, we pulled up at the hotel just after the sun had set.

An extra day was spent at Tarbes to thoroughly clean the motor, and, as it rained most of the time, we were not sorry that we were delayed.

The next day we made an early start for Lourdes. We arrived about ten, the place was fairly full of pilgrims, although the greater number go there in the month of August. It is a beautiful spot, the town itself being small, principally composed of shops selling relics and souvenirs to the visitors. An imposing church has been erected over the grotto, where the peasant girl, Bernadette Souvivon, was said to have seen the Virgin. The photograph shews the grotto, where both inside and on the left of it, can be seen the crutches of those who have been cured of their lameness.

From Lourdes to Pau the road ran parallel to the river Save du Pau.

The hills rise at once from the river's edge, the lower hills crowned with trees and brushwood, while beyond them in the background towered the Pyrenees covered with snow. The effect was very fine. All the villages we passed through seemed most prosperous, probably chiefly due to the enormous number of pilgrims who annually make their journey to Lourdes.

We lunched at Pau and later continued our journey to Biarritz. Biarritz needs no description and has no doubt many attractions, but for a winter resort I should say San Sebastian is much pleasanter. Its harbour is completely sheltered from the storms of the Atlantic, the beach is sandy and excellent for bathing and undoubtedly it is one of the most beautifully situated seaports. The hotels are first rate and most of the attendants speak French, and a few English. A week passed quickly enough, and again we were on the road for Bordeaux. We lunched at Mont-de-Mersan, in the Hotel Richelieu, I mention the name as it was quite the best lunch we had on our travels.

We burst a tyre soon after leaving Mont-de-Mersan, perhaps the excellent lunch had something to do with it. It took us the best part of an hour to replace, but once again on the move we were once not long arriving at Bordeaux.

We were not particularly interested in the town so left the following day. Soon after starting we were stopped by an accident. A man had jumped out of a runaway trap and was lying unconscious by the roadside. Fortunately we had a flask with us, and gave him some brandy, the chauffeur took the car to the nearest village to fetch a doctor. Meanwhile the runaway trap returned, and, as soon as the wretched man recovered they began to abuse him for jumping out! A crowd meanwhile had collected, and not wishing to be mixed up in the accident, we left, being warmly thanked for our help by the owner of the trap.

Putting on speed to reach Angouleme before dark another tyre burst; this was becoming tiresome, but both the tyres that had burst had each done over 3,000 miles so there was no reason to complain. I think it is excessive speed that uses them up quickly.

Personally I dislike fast driving on roads. Let alone extra wear and tear to the car generally, and being a nuisance to your fellow people, one cannot half appreciate the beauties of the country you are travelling through. We spent the night at Angouleme, and the following at Chatellerault.

On our way to Tours we passed through the quaint little village of Richelieu the birthplace of the great Cardinal.

We were now approaching the chateaux country; Baedeker, or any guidebook gives a complete description of them all, so I will not enlarge! About 5 pm we approached Tours and soon after pulled up at the Hotel de l'Univers which was comfortable, but expensive.

Tours is an excellent centre for visiting the Chateaux, and a week is none too long a time to devote to the study of these interesting places. It is a mistake to attempt to see too many chateaux, or do more than three in one day, or even to sight-see daily, for, not to mention the fatigue, one's impressions are apt to become jumbled and inaccurate.

We found the historical Chateaux of Blois, Chenonceaux, Chaumont and Loches the most fascinating, but there are others, as perfectly restored, and to see the rooms decorated and furnished, as when used originally, gives a vivid picture of those times.

From Tours we went to Orleans and, after dining there, drove by night to Paris, where we spent a week, and then continued our journey to Cherbourg, by way of Evereaux, Lisieux and Caen, the last named having a very beautiful cathedral, built by William the Conqueror, and at Lisieux is the famous tapestry, worked and designed by his wife Matilda, representing the conquest of England by her Royal spouse. The figures and scenes depicted on it are most quaint and amusing, and, when Napoleon I wanted recruits for the invasion of England, he had this tapestry taken to Paris and exhibited there.

From Cherbourg we returned to Caen and so on to Dieppe by Rouen also passing along the coast by the fashionable French watering places of Leon-sur-Mer, Houlgate, Trouville etc.

This part of our route, although very pretty and interesting, was unpleasantly crowded with motors. The dust they raised never seemed to settle, and inclined one to think how detestable every motor except one's own was! We spent the night at Dieppe which was packed to overflowing, this decided us to cross over the following day to England, which we did, and thus concluded our most delightful tour in France.

G. L.

GENERAL BIBLIOGRAPHY

Introduction

A total of four books were published by Ediciones del Genal of Málaga in 2014 and 2015 about the hotel and George. None is currently available in English:

Enciso, C. & Navas, E. *George Langworthy y Santa Clara. Pioneros de la Costa del Sol* (Ediciones del Genal of Málaga, 2014). This is a brief biography of George's life supplemented by a collection of photographs.

Enciso, C. & Navas, E. *El Hotel del Inglés* (Ediciones del Genal of Málaga, 2014). This is a novel recounting the conversion of the fort into a home, then a hotel and its fate after George's death.

Valle de Juan, M.A. & Beautell González, C. *El Hotel Santa Clara y Mistress Beautell* (Ediciones del Genal of Málaga, 2015). This is the account of the involvement of the Beautell family in the initial development of the hotel.

'Comunidad de Proprietarios La Cornisa de Santa Clara Torremolinos' *El Castillo de Santa Clara. Un Lugar Emblemático* (Ediciones del Genal of Málaga, 2015). This is a publication of papers about the current and past hotel presented at a conference in August 2014 organised by owners of property in the building which replaced George's.

Chapter One

Torres, R. *El cementerio de los Ingleses* (Ediciones Xorki, 2015) recounts the story of the cemetery and lists its 'occupants' and the stories of some of them. Not available in English.

Chapter Two

https://rusholmearchive.org/langdalethe-home-of-edward-langworthy

Bergin, T., Pearce, D. N., Shaw, S. *Salford: A City and Its Past* (City of Salford Cultural Services Department, 1975).

Engels, F. *Condition of the Working Class in England* (Panther Edition, 1969), see https://www.marxists.org/archive/marx/works/download/pdf/condition-working-class-england.pdf

www.manchester.ac.uk/the-langworthy-story/

Grace's Guide to British Industrial Industry, see https://www.gracesguide.co.uk/1891

Chapter Three

Information and quotations in this chapter come mainly from the following sources:

Matthews, B. *By God's Grace. A History of Uppingham School.* (Hutchinson, 1984)

Rudman, J. *A Dateline History* (unpublished).

Additional material is from Tozer, M. *The Ideal of Manliness: The Legacy of Thring's Uppingham* (Sunnyrest Books, 2015).

Chapter Four

The information and quotations in this chapter come from:

Gunn, S. *The Public Culture of the Victorian Middle Class* (Manchester University Press, 2000).

Huggins, M. and Mangan, J. (eds.) *Disreputable Pleasures* (Routledge, 2004)

Professor Gunn informed me verbally that Friedrich Engels was a member of the Lyme Harriers. The estate is now in the hands of the National Trust, who told me that no records of the hunt are at Lyme.

Chapter Five

Robinson, W. S. *Muckraker. The Scandalous Life and Times of W. T. Stead* (The Robson Press, 2013).

Robinson devotes five pages to the Langworthy affair and I draw on his observations about Stead and the case in this chapter. Other material is drawn from the Internet.

Copies of the *Pall Mall Gazette* are freely available on the Internet at British Library Newspapers, see http://tinyurl.galegroup.com/tinyurl/.

Mulhall, M. G. & E. T. *Handbook of the River Plate* (Kegan, Paul, Trench & Co., 6th ed., 1892).

Chapter Six

This chapter is informed by three books (especially De Courcy) plus the archive of the Royal Dragoons Museum at York, and the Internet.

Churchill, W. S. *My Early Life. A Roving Commission.* (Macmillan & Co.) A digital copy is accessible on the Internet.

De Courcy, A. *The Fishing Fleet. Husband – Hunting in the Raj* (Weidenfeld & Nicholson, 2012)

Holmes R. *Sahib. The British Soldier in India 1750-1914.* (Harper Press, 2005)

The *Black Horse Gazette* is the journal of the 7th Dragoon Guards and provided both general information and specific news about George.

Chapter Seven

Information in this chapter is gleaned from the Internet and the *Black Horse Gazette.* Additional guidance and information came from Belinda Day, senior curator, Collections Development and Review, the National Army Museum; and from Revd. Peter Kettle, assistant priest, Holy Trinity, Prince Consort Road, Knightsbridge.

Chapter Eight

Speculation as to where the couple might live after the wedding is informed by the fact that in her will, dated 1903, Annie's bequests included two of George's relatives: his brother John and his cousin Florence, the unfortunate only sister of the ill-fated Edward Martin Langworthy (EML). Florence lived near Maidenhead in Berkshire, less that forty miles by road and well served by trains from Oxford. John lived in Lymington, Hampshire, a similar distance from Annie's childhood home with the Revd. Penny near Blandford Forum in Dorset. In May 1900, newspapers carried the announcement of Annie's father's intention to marry a Mrs Charles Reid in the autumn of that year, though she is not in residence at the Oxford house, 1 Holywell Street, on the day of the 1901 census when Annie is living there.

Publication of the *Black Horse Gazette* was suspended after the regiment joined the British forces in the Boer War. Publication resumed in 1906 and carried a series of articles entitled 'Reminiscences of the War in South Africa from 1900–1902' which provided much information for this chapter.

I also consulted the official British government account of the war, Maurice, Sir John Frederick; Grant, Maurice Harold, *History of the War in South Africa, 1899–1902* (British War Office, four volumes, 1906–1910). Here I learned of the regiment's casualties:

Killed or died of wounds: 3 officers, 20 men.

Died of disease: 34 men.

Wounded: 8 officers (George amongst them, of course), 54 men.

Captured by the enemy: 54 men.

Additional material came from the Internet plus,

Nasson, B. *The South African War 1899–1902* (Edward Arnold Publishers, 1999).

Chapter Nine

This chapter draws on a variety of sources, including the internet, the Black Horse Gazette, the four books in Spanish cited above in the notes for the Foreword, plus verbal information kindly given by Remi Fernandez Campoy, the daughter of Maria Campoy who studied at George's expense and worked for him .

Additional material comes from:

Chislett, W. *Spain, What Everyone Needs to Know* (Oxford University Press, 2013)

Grocott, C. and Stockey, G. *Gibraltar: A Modern History* (University of Wales Press, 2012).

Harris, M. C. *A Corner of Spain* (1898) a facsimile hard copy is available from Bibliolife (www.bibliolife.com/opensource) but a digital copy can also be found on the Internet

Sharman, N. 'Spain and Britain's Informal Empire' in Grady, J. and Grocott, C. (eds) *The Continuing Imperialism of Free Trade* (Routledge, 2019).

Walton, J. K. 'British Perceptions of Spain and their Impact on Attitudes to the Spanish Civil War' in *Twentieth Century British History*, vol. 5., No. 3, (1994) pp. 283–99.

Gareth Stockey (associate professor, University of Nottingham) kindly gave me additional information verbally.

Chapter Ten

Again, the four books in Spanish cited above in the bibliography for the introduction provided material for this chapter supplemented by verbal information from the descendants of Margaret Beautell (née Horn) as well as Remi Fernandez Campoy.

Chapter Eleven

Many books have been written by both Spaniards and foreigners about the Spanish Civil War, a complex subject which is still the focus of debate and controversy.

One of the best English authorities is Paul Preston, whose *The Spanish Holocaust* (Harper Collins, 2012) informed this chapter. His other books on the Civil War, on Franco and on King Juan Carlos are all highly regarded.

There are books on the war containing eye-witness accounts, one of which, in English, was first published in 1979 then re-printed in 1986 to mark the fiftieth anniversary of the start of the war: Fraser, R. *Blood of Spain* (Pantheon Books, 1979). A recent book published only in Spanish is *Yo Estaba Allí [I Was There]* (Ediciones del Genal, 2016) based on interviews with survivors of the war aged between eighty-five and 104.

I have chosen to draw primarily on sources in the immediate area of Torremolinos. Gamel Woolsey and Gerald Brenan lived in Churriana which is now a western suburb of Málaga quite close to the airport. Their house (Casa Gerald Brenan) on the Calle Torremolinos is now a museum, but there are not many artefacts in it, though it is used for talk and presentations linked to Brenan. Sir Peter Chalmers-Mitchell lived in Málaga itself. He was instantly recognisable on the streets of the city as he always wore a white suit.

Woolsey, G. *Death's Other Kingdom* (Virago, 1988). This was originally published in 1939 and was re-published as *Málaga Burning* in 1998 by Pythia Press of Reston, Virginia. The original title was a quotation from a poem by T. S. Eliot, but was regarded as too obscure for the re-publication. In 1997 a Spanish translation, *Málaga en Llamas [Málaga in Flames]* was published by Temas de Hoy of Barcelona.

Her husband, Gerald Brenan, was highly regarded by Spaniards. His books include *The Spanish Labyrinth* (1943) regarded by many as the most perceptive study of modern Spain available at the time. He donated his body to the University of Málaga for research, though some say it was to avoid the cost of a funeral. However he was so revered that no-one would dissect the body, so it was finally cremated and the ashes interred in the British cemetery in Málaga alongside Gamel.

Chalmers-Mitchell, P. *My House in Málaga* (Faber & Faber, 1937). Clapton Press of London published a paperback version in May 2019. It is a fascinating account of a generous man who believed his nationality protected him from danger, up until a certain time.

Chapter Thirteen

Much information in this chapter is gleaned from the Internet, but some other English language publications are referenced and detailed below. There are several websites celebrating Torremolinos and containing many photos and reminiscences. They include:

https://andaluciainformacion.es/torremolinos
http://memories-of-torremolinos.blogspot.com/
http://www.torremolinoschic.com/
Torremolinos en Imágenes (A Facebook group)

A Spanish publication of value in this chapter is:

Arenas, A. & Majada, J. *Viajeros y Turistas en la Costa del Sol [Travellers and Tourists on the Costa del Sol]* (Editorial Miramar, 2003).

English language titles:

Grice-Hutchinson, M., *Málaga Farm*. It was published in 2001 in Spanish as *Un Cortijo en Málaga* (Editorial Agora, 1956).

Lee, L. (1969) *As I Walked Out One Midsummer Morning* (Penguin Books, 1971). Originally published by Andre Deutsch.

Macaulay, R. *Fabled Shore* (Oxford University Press, 1949; paperback, 1986).

Michener, J. A. *The Drifters* (Corgi, 1972).